THE COMPLETE CATALOGUE
OF THE
AUSTIN SEVEN

All Austin Seven variants from around the world, 1922-1939

By James Taylor

Herridge & Sons

Photography credits
Simon Clay, Austin Seven Club's Association, Motorsport Images, Matthew Barker, Clive Barker, Mal Barker (Cars Down Under), Nick Turley, Robin Lawton (www.robinlawton.com), RS Vintage (www.rsvintage.co.uk), Dickon Armstrong, David Hodges Collection, Robert Knight, Mike Tebbett

Published 2023 by
Herridge & Sons Ltd
Lower Forda, Shebbear
Beaworthy, Devon
EX21 5SY

ISBN 978-1-914929-07-6
Printed in China

CONTENTS

INTRODUCTION & ACKNOWLEDGEMENTS

A classic Austin Seven Chummy. This is a 1928 Type AD Tourer. (Simon Clay)

The Austin Seven was a hugely important arrival on the British motoring scene in 1922, its low price making car ownership available to a section of the public for whom this had earlier been a cost too far. It was cheap to run thanks to its small engine, and its simplicity did not frighten those new to the mechanics of a car. The Seven heralded the demise of the cheap but flimsy cyclecar, and in the longer term it also attracted buyers away from the motorcycle-and-sidecar combinations that had been the only way into motorised transport for those of limited means.

A century after the Seven's introduction, the cars have a world-wide following. Part of the attraction is much the same as it always was – simplicity of maintenance and the low cost of ownership. Yet the sheer variety of Sevens produced between 1922 and 1939 as Austin gradually developed the model is also a source

A 1937 ACA Pearl Cabriolet. This one was actually built in Berlin by Willys Overland Crossley. (Matthew Barker)

of fascination – and of some bewilderment and confusion.

There have been several erudite tomes about the Seven over the years, and Bob Wyatt's *Austin Seven* (which first appeared in 1968) and Bryan Purves' *Austin Seven Source Book* (first published in 1989) remain indispensable building blocks for the study and understanding of the Seven. There is still more to be discovered about the story of these cars, but the present volume is not intended to present further research. Rather is it intended to resume what is currently known in a convenient and readily-accessible catalogue form.

It would be wonderful to be able to illustrate every single model of Austin Seven in a single book, but on current evidence that is an impossibility. In some cases, pictures either do not exist or are simply too expensive to buy in. The illustrations in this book have come from a wide variety of sources, but I must particularly single out photographer Simon Clay, the British Motor Industry Trust (which holds the Austin archives) and the many individuals who have generously made their photographs available through online media.

Thanks must also go to The Austin Seven Club's Association and its committee and registrars. To have such experts on hand has been invaluable. In particular, I must thank Mike Costigan, Chris Garner, Ruairidh Dunford, Tom Abernethy, Nick Turley, Mike Tebbett, Michael Brodribb and Hugh Barnes.

James Taylor
Oxfordshire
April 2023

OVERVIEW

Austin chose to enter the post-war period with a one-model policy, and the model they settled on was the Twenty. Introduced in 1919, this robust car was fairly typical Austin fare, and it sold well in Australia as well as at home. However, the boom that followed the end of the Great War was short-lived, and all too soon the UK was plunged into a deep recession. In these conditions, sales of cars like the Twenty collapsed, and the imposition in 1921 of a vehicle excise duty that cost £1 annually for every RAC-rated horsepower made matters worse. By the end of the year, Austin was in trouble and a receiver was appointed early in 1922. Fortunately, the rapid development of a smaller Twelve model and its introduction in November 1921 helped to stave off bankruptcy.

Chairman and founder Sir Herbert Austin came to believe that only an even smaller car, cheap enough to appeal to a wider sector of the public, would guarantee the future of his company. According to legend, he produced full-size sketches of his early thoughts on the design of such a car at his home of Lickey Grange, near Bromsgrove, in the billiards room (although not, as is commonly suggested, on the billiards table itself!). The other Austin Directors were not keen on the idea of making a car smaller than their Twelve, but Austin decided to pursue his vision in his own time and at his own expense.

By the time of the Seven, Herbert Austin had become Sir Herbert, knighted for his services to the nation during the 1914-1918 war. He was also an MP, for the Birmingham King's Norton ward.

To help him with the work, he secured the services of a talented young draughtsman from the Longbridge factory. Stanley Edge had started work in the Austin drawing office in 1917 when aged just 14, and had been transferred to the car section at the end of the war. Austin's early thoughts focused on a car that shared some features with the 1919 Rover Eight, a light car designed by Jack Sangster of Ariel motor cycle fame with an air-cooled horizontally-opposed twin-cylinder engine. However, the car that eventually emerged was altogether more conventional, with a 696cc four-cylinder engine.

Stanley Edge had a very large hand in its design. Unfamiliarity with some of the components led him to draw them as scaled-down versions of those already in production for Austin's larger cars, and in this way the new small car became a downsized and simplified version of what might be called "real" cars rather than a cheap and cheerful cyclecar like so many contemporary products at the lower end of the market. Austin astutely patented some of the new car's features as they came off the drawing-board, which enabled him to take a royalty of two guineas (£2 2s 0d) for every Austin Seven made once the car had entered production.

That shrewd move did not go unnoticed by Austin's fellow Directors. Concerned that he might take his ideas elsewhere if they proved successful, they agreed to the construction of prototypes at the Longbridge factory. The first two cars were shown to the Austin workers and their families at the factory's Whitsun Carnival on 4-5th June 1922. An improved third car was ready by the summer. Austin was impatient to announce the new model and chose not to wait for the Olympia Motor Show in November. Instead, he arranged for the new car to be launched to the press at London's Claridges Hotel on 21st July.

There was a certain amount of scepticism about the new Austin at first, and the £225 asking price was a little optimistic. By the end of the year, only about 2000 orders had been taken (although production had not started until November and deliveries did not begin until the start of 1923). Herbert Austin realised his mistake, and dropped the price to £165 in December 1923. That helped, and for Austin it was a lesson well learned. Throughout most of the history of the Seven, showroom prices would be lowered whenever manufacturing costs allowed it, and there can be no doubt that this value-for-money approach made a significant contribution to the model's success.

All the first cars were four-seat Tourers, with just one door on each side and a folding hood to give protection against the elements. This was entirely in keeping with public expectations at the time: the day when the enclosed Saloon would become the norm was still some years away. There was not a great deal of room in the body for four people, and before long the little Austin, like other close-couple four seaters, gained the popular nickname of "Chummy" – because the four occupants had to be good chums if they were to travel very far in it.

Austin kept an eye on customer reactions, of course, and developed improvements to improve the car's appeal. First came an enlarged engine of 747cc in 1923, and then a slightly enlarged body the following summer, while wider tyres and a speedometer as standard were the changes for 1925. There were some other changes, too, partly no doubt to simplify production – and Austin passed on to the customers the savings they made in manufacturing, by gradually reducing prices.

Pictures of the prototype Sevens in their original state are rare. This is the only known one showing the second car, XL2

While the Tourer was still securing its place in the hearts of British car buyers, Austin followed up with a second model. This time, it was a small Delivery Van, which was aimed at a very different group of customers from the Tourer and in that sense was a shrewd move.

The early engines depended on a magneto, and had no cooling fan. This one dates from 1924.

There is near-global appreciation of the Seven's place in motoring history today, and the 100th anniversary of its birth was celebrated by the Austin Seven Clubs Association in 2022. (Matthew Barker)

Austin wanted as broad a customer base for the car as he could achieve in order to build up production volumes. However, he also wanted to ensure that he did not tie up manufacturing resources in a venture that was, initially at least, speculative. So, although the design of the Van was done at the Austin works, its manufacture was sub-contracted to Startin, a commercial bodybuilder in Birmingham. The first examples reached their buyers during 1923.

Simplicity was always key, and the early Seven bonnet was a three-piece assembly that simply lifted off.

In the mean time, the little Austin had also made its debut in motor sport, where many events ran classes specifically for small-engined cars. First off the mark was Gordon England, who told Sir Herbert quite bluntly that "the only way to make the public accept the Austin Seven was to race it from the beginning." Intrigued, Austin summoned England to a meeting and agreed to let him have a chassis to try out his ideas, and the result was campaigned at Brooklands with some success. Austin's own son-in-law, Arthur Waite, shared England's opinion that racing might attract some valuable publicity for the still-new model. By the spring of 1923, he had prepared a racing Seven which he took to Brooklands, and later that year he took it to first place at an event held at Monza in Italy. A small racing department already existed at Austin and three cars were campaigned with somewhat mixed fortunes during 1924.

By 1924, according to a 1935 issue of the *Austin Magazine*, the Seven had won "no fewer than fifty-five events and awards." The stage was set for some sporting production derivatives, and in fact the first of them was

Multiple different body styles, including those by coachbuilders, appeared as sales increased. This Two-Seater was bodied by Swallow, a company that went on to become a car manufacturer itself, first as SS and later as Jaguar. (Clive Barker)

announced in January 1924. Its name of "50mph Sports" sounds amusing today, but in those days a guaranteed 50mph from such a small car was a thing of some wonder. This now left the Austin Seven available in three guises – Tourer, Delivery Van, and Sports – and of course Austin were only too pleased to supply bare chassis as well for owners to have bodied by their own favoured coachbuilder. It was these bare chassis that led on to some more important developments in the story of the Austin Seven.

Gordon England (he of the Brooklands racer) had decided to set himself up as a coachbuilder and to concentrate on the smaller chassis that were now becoming popular. The established grand coachbuilders were too expensive for all but the very wealthy, which left a space for England, and others like him, to fill. Crucially, he recognised that weight would be an issue for a small-engined chassis like the Seven, and he put his experience with aircraft manufacture to good use in designing bodies that would not over-tax the car.

On the one hand, he created lightweight sporting two-seaters that appealed to those with a liking for speed, and his Brooklands Super Sports of 1924 came with a certificate guaranteeing an 80mph top speed – which seemed almost fantastical in comparison with the 50mph promised by Austin's own Sports model. On the other, he used his lightweight construction methods to take the weight out of a Saloon body, and by the end of 1925 he had one ready to go. During 1927, he had also introduced a Delivery Van to compete with the standard Austin offering.

The success of these models, which were of course built on chassis obtained from the Austin works, must have made Herbert Austin sit up and take notice. However, instead of considering the Gordon England models as a threat, he decided on a more pragmatic approach. He agreed to promote the Sports models and Saloons in his own catalogues (where he pointed out quite clearly that responsibility for their bodies lay entirely with the Gordon England concern); the existing contract with Startin probably prevented him from including the Delivery Vans as well. He also set his designers to work on a Saloon model that Austin would build themselves, and had it ready by April 1926. With aluminium panels on a traditional ash frame, it was not as light as the Gordon England models, but it was very much less

Sales brochures in the mid-1920s extolled the virtues of the Seven in several different ways. This 1926 example focuses on its appeal to women drivers....

... and this one from the same year presents the car in quite a different light.

expensive.

By the end of 1926, Austin had built 25,000 Sevens, and had begun exporting the model overseas as well. This led on naturally to enquiries from overseas about licence manufacture, and during 1927 the first licence was granted to the Dixi company in Germany. Two years later, Dixi would be bought out by aero engine maker BMW, and the BMW Dixi became the first in a long line of successful cars from the Bavarian manufacturer. In 1928, Rosengart in France took out a licence, and in 1930 the American Austin Company was formed in the USA to build what became familiarly known as the Bantam. American Austin later became American Bantam, and in 1940 designed the vehicle that would enter production as the military Jeep.

Output of Austin Sevens continued to expand. The 50,000th car was made in November 1927, and by the end of the decade the figure stood at 100,000. In 1930, Austin built 23,826 Sevens, which represented well over half their total output for that year of 43,000 vehicles. Up to 1927, the Seven had been Britain's cheapest "real" car, but in that year Triumph introduced its Super Seven, and in 1928 Morris introduced the first Minor. Both were direct competitors for the Austin Seven, and from now on Austin had to keep one eye on what his rivals were doing in order to keep his Seven competitive.

In the mean time, yet another body type had been added to the Austin factory's output of Tourers, Sports, Delivery Vans (whose manufacture was taken in-house in 1930) and Saloons. This time, it was a Coupé, although unlike the earlier "Doctor's Coupé", the car that became available in 1928 looked actually like a four-seater saloon (although there was no real rear seat, more of an upholstered shelf) with blind rear quarters. It never met the same success as the other factory-built types, and was actually withdrawn from sale after only two years.

As public demand for Saloon models increased, so that for open cars gradually declined, and one result of this was that Austin decided to see whether a new model that combined elements of the Sports models with elements of the Tourer would attract buyers. In 1929, he tested the market with a stylish model that was described simply as a Two-seater, and this proved sufficiently popular to remain in the Seven range right through the following decade.

Interestingly, the Two-seater was always more about style and fashion than about practicality, and yet in the early 1930s its descendants would be chosen by the British Army for reconnaissance duties.

The turn of the decade marked a watershed of sorts in the story of the Austin Seven. Sales were not immune to the impact of the 1929 Wall Street Crash and the Depression that followed, but Austin's small car suffered less than many more expensive models as money became tight. Some Austin Seven enthusiasts consider the cars that came after 1930 as a rather different breed from the original models of the 1920s, but they had simply changed to meet the requirements and tastes of their times – and that competition from rivals.

For the first few years of the 1930s, the Seven was visually much as it had been before, but a change in emphasis was already discernible. Tourers remained available, but the public was increasingly turning to Saloon models. Sports models remained in the range, too, but gradually became more refined as buyers rejected the idea that performance had to be associated with discomfort. The Delivery Vans carried on much as before, changing only as the parent chassis changed and now, of course, built by Austin themselves. A few companies continued to offer alternatives to the factory-built models, but the great age of the special-bodied Austin Seven was over, as the Depression had wiped out most of the smaller coachbuilders who had produced such cars.

The first set of changes began as early as 1930. The Saloons changed from aluminium bodywork to steel, giving some reduction in manufacturing costs. Much more important for the longer term was that the Seven quite literally grew up. It had been clear for a long time that the 75-inch wheelbase chassis with which the car had been introduced in 1923 restricted space in the body to an unacceptable degree, and as a result it was redesigned with another six inches to give an 81-inch dimension. The Seven remained a small car, but it was now better equipped to counter its rivals. At about the same time, a coupled braking system became standard, allowing both front and rear brakes to be operated by the foot pedal for the first time.

The next changes affected the mechanical components, and in particular the gearbox. In September 1932, the old three-speed box gave way to a four-speed type; a year later,

This slightly later engine had gained a belt-driven cooling fan but its crankshaft still had only two bearings.

Austin were clearly proud of the Seven and created displays to showcase its simplicity. This 1929 show chassis was-painted in pale-blue…

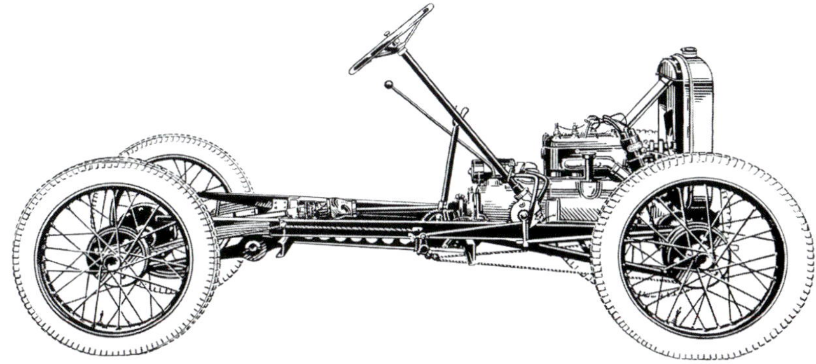

… and this is an illustration from a 1931 sales catalogue. The point, perhaps, was to show that there was no mechanical complexity to frighten the would-be owner.

Not just simple, but strong, too.... another catalogue illustration shows very clearly the layout of the front suspension.

When writing ALWAYS quote the ENGINE NUMBER

Austin Seven

Pump Engine

LIST OF SPARE PARTS

Publication No. 1707

The AUSTIN MOTOR CO. LTD., LONGBRIDGE :: BIRMINGHAM ENGLAND

Austin seized other opportunities to make the most of their baby car. This spare parts list is for a version of its engine adapted to power a pump.

synchromesh was added on third and fourth gears; and then in 1934 synchromesh spread to cover second gear as well. Two years after that, it was the turn of the engine, which gained a third (white-metalled) crankshaft bearing to the benefit of both smoothness and durability.

However, the most obvious change to the Seven came in 1934, when the entire body was redesigned, along with the front end panels. This was the age of the Ruby Saloon, the Pearl Cabriolet and the Opal Tourer, which in their turn became just as highly regarded – loved, even – as the models of the preceding decade. With relatively minor improvements, these were the models that carried the range through to its end in 1939. Yet even Sir Herbert Austin acknowledged that they represented the passing of an era when he introduced the new models to the press at Longbridge in August: "Whilst I appreciate the advances these new model represent," he said, "it is not without a tinge of regret that I see the passing of our familiar radiator shell which has been associated with the name of Austin since the founding of the firm."

In fact, not every version of the Seven took on the new radiator shell, and the Opal Two-seater retained the old flat-fronted type. It also became the first car in Austin's history to be priced at exactly £100, which made it something of a

Delivery Vans figured in the catalogues for the Seven from the earliest times. By the time this one was printed in 1934, they were being assembled at the Austin factory rather than under contract elsewhere – but it was policy for them to use up stocks of parts for earlier models!

This is the later front-end style on a Ruby saloon. The model name remained clearly emblazoned on the grille with its painted metal surround, and of course the winged Austin emblem surmounted the whole.

The new front end design introduced in 1934 gave the little Austin a quite different appearance, and yet the car somehow always looked friendly and welcoming.

bargain. However, keeping showroom prices down was becoming ever more necessary as the Seven came under increasing pressure from its rivals, all of which were fundamentally newer designs. The new models delivered a welcome boost to sales in 1935, but annual figures began to slide after that. In 1938 there was some hasty reshuffling of prices to keep the range competitive with offerings in the same price bracket from Ford.

By then, Sir Herbert had already concluded that competition in the baby-car market was too fierce to be sustainable, and the flow of new models now dried up. The Sports models were the first to go, and when the last examples of the existing type were built in summer 1937, they were not replaced. Meanwhile, July 1937 saw Austin introduce the first "Big Seven", an entirely new car with a larger four-door Saloon body and a larger 900cc engine. He told the press that this was an addition to the Austin family and that it would not replace the existing Seven, but a cheaper version announced in March 1938 suggested that, at the very least, plans had now changed.

Production of the original Seven begin to wind up as most models came to an end in January 1939, and the following month Austin introduced its new Eight model in order to compete more effectively in the market. The last

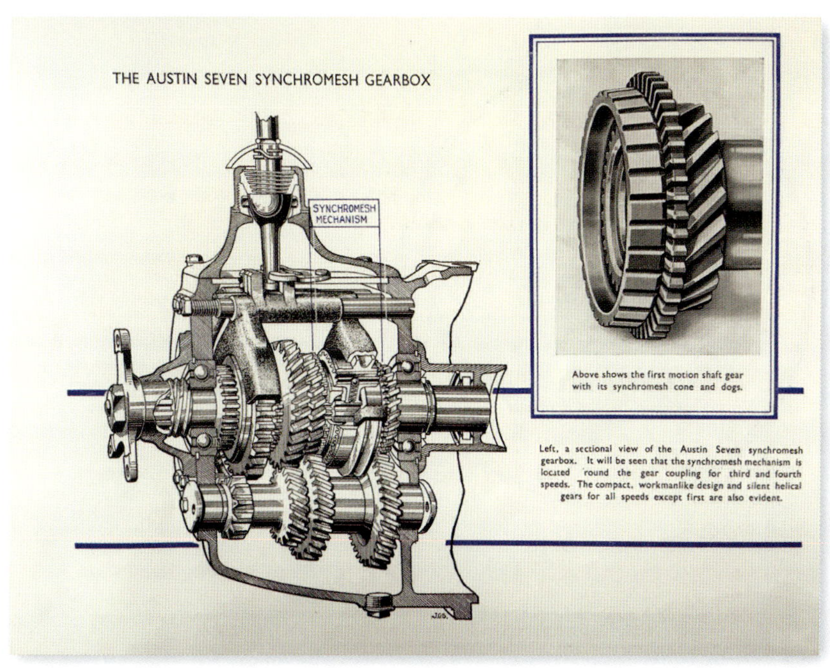

Gradual improvements over the years brought the addition of synchromesh. Here, it has been introduced on third and fourth gears, but a year later second gear would also have it.

Seven models in production were Delivery Vans, and Austin continued to build these until July 1939, perhaps in anticipation of replacing them with a derivative of the new Eight or perhaps the Big Seven later in the year. Their end came just before Europe was plunged into war with Nazi Germany, and the cars that began to leave the Longbridge production lines six years later would face a very different world from the one that the little Seven had known.

More gradual improvements, and this time to the engine, which gained a third main bearing in 1936.

AUSTIN SEVEN PRODUCTION, 1922-1939

These are the generally accepted annual production figures for the Austin Seven.

1922	178	1931	20,645
1923	2409	1932	21,285
1924	4800	1933	20,383
1925	8024	1934	22,685
1926	13,174	1935	27,225
1927	21,671	1936	24,523
1928	24,247	1937	20,671
1929	26,540	1938	8089
1930	23,739	1939	656

A round figure of 290,000 is generally agreed as the total for Austin Seven production (the figures above actually total 290,944).

KEY DATES ON THE AUSTIN SEVEN TIMELINE

1922, July	Austin Seven announced
1923, March	Engine size from 696cc to 747cc
1923, November	Electric starter fitted
1924, January	50mph Sports introduced
1925, August	Gordon England Cup model introduced
1926, March	Balloon tyres standardised
1926, April	First factory-built Saloon
1926, September	Headlamps from scuttle to front wings (some models briefly reverted to scuttle-mounted lamps). Four-piece bonnet replaces three-piece type
1928, August	Nickelled radiator shell
1928, September	Coil ignition replaces magneto type
1929, October	Ball-type gear change
1930, July	Coupled front and rear brakes
1931	Longer wheelbase
1932, September	Four-speed gearbox replaces three-speed type
1934, July	First models of redesigned range, now with "jewel" names: Ruby (July), Pearl and Opal (August)
1936, June	Three-bearing engine replaces two-bearing type
1938, June	Girling rod brakes
1939, July	Final production of Austin Seven (most models ended production in March)

WHAT WAS AVAILABLE AND WHEN?

The sheer number of different Austin Seven models can be confusing, so the table that follows is an attempt to ease that confusion by showing on a calender-year basis which models were available. Note that calendar-year and model-year (or season) were not at all the same thing. New models were often introduced mid-way through the year, with the result that both old and new models fell into the same calendar-year.

For further clarification of the type codes, please see the later table.

YEAR	MODELs
1922	Tourer: Type A
1923	Tourer: Type A, Type B Delivery Van: Type B (Startin)
1924	Tourer: Type B, Type C Delivery Van: Type B, Type C Startin) Sports: 50mph Sports
1925	Tourer: Type C ,Delivery Van: Type C (Startin) Sports: 50mph Sports, Sports Two-seater Coupé
1926	Tourer: Type C, Type D Delivery Van: Type C, Type D (Startin) Sports: 50mph Sports Saloon: Type R
1927	Tourer: Type D Delivery Van: Type D (Startin) Sports: Super Sports Type E Saloon: Type R, Type RF
1928	Tourer: Type D (AD) Delivery Van: Type AE (Startin) Sports: Super Sports Type E Saloon: Type R, Type RK Coupé: Type B
1929	Tourer: Type AD, Type AE Delivery Van: Type AE (Startin) Sports: Super Sports Type E Saloon: Type RK Coupé: Type B Two-seater: Type P, Type PA
1930	Tourer: Type AE, Type AF Delivery Van: Type AE, Type AF (Startin), Type VD Milk Delivery: Type VC Sports: Super Sports Type E, Type EA (Ulster) Saloon: Type RF, Type RG, Type RL Coupé: Type B Two-seater: Type P, Type PA
1931	Tourer: Type AF, Type AG Delivery Van: Type VD, Type VG Milk Delivery: Type MDC Sports: Type EA (Ulster) Saloon: Type RG, Type RH, Type RM Two-seater: Type PB, Type PC

YEAR	MODELs
1932	Tourer: Type AG, Type AH Delivery Van: Type VG Sports: Type EA (Ulster) Saloon: Type RM, Type RN, Type RP Two-seater: Type PC
1933	Tourer: Type AH Delivery Van: Type VG, Type AVH Sports: Type EB Saloon: Type RP Two-seater: Type PD
1934	Tourer: Type AH, Type AAK Delivery Van: Type AVH Sports: Type EB, Type EK, Type AEB Saloon: Type RP, Type ARQ Two-seater: Type PD, Type APD Cabriolet: Type AC
1935	Tourer: Type AAK Delivery Van: Type AVH, Type AVJ Sports: Type AEB, Type AEK Saloon: Type ARQ Two-seater: Type APD, Type APE Cabriolet: Type AC
1936	Tourer: Type AAK, Type AAL Delivery Van: Type AVJ Sports: Type AEB, Type AEK Saloon: Type AEQ, Type ARR Two-seater: Type APE Cabriolet: Type AC
1937	Tourer: Type AAL Delivery Van: Type AVJ, Type AVK Sports: Type AEB Saloon: Type ARR Two-seater: Type APE Cabriolet: Type ACA
1938	Tourer: Type AAL Delivery Van: Type AVK Saloon: Type ARR Two-seater: Type APE Cabriolet: Type ACA
1939	Tourer: Type AAL Delivery Van: Type AVK Saloon: Type ARR Two-seater: Type APE Cabriolet: Type ACA

THE EARLY MODELS 1922-1926

The very first Austin Seven models sold to the public were all four-seat Tourers. Austin built their bodies in-house at their Longbridge factory, using the traditional coachbuilding method of attaching aluminium panels to an ash framework.

These cars had the 747cc engine with 10.5bhp, a three-speed gearbox with no synchromesh, and the propellor shaft to the rear axle ran through a torque tube. With a top speed of 50mph in the right conditions, the early Sevens were not quick, but they had performance enough to delight most buyers at the time.

The engine had no cooling fan at first, and it was provided with a detachable starting handle, although a mechanical starter was an optional extra and an electric starter was made standard in December 1923. Fuel was stored in a four-gallon tank mounted on the scuttle, and instrumentation was minimal; there was an electrical switchbox on the dashboard but early cars had no speedometer. All four wheels had brakes, but the handbrake worked only on the front wheels and the footbrake on the rears.

Austin was constantly looking for ways to improve the Seven, and there were several changes during the first few years of production that affected all the models that were in production at the time. From November 1923, a belt-driven two-bladed cooling fan was fitted after some cars had suffered from engine overheating during the summer. A speedometer was made available as an option in February 1924. The suspension was improved by adding Hartford friction-type shock absorbers shortly after that, firstly to the front axle and later to the rear.

From February 1925 well-base 19in wheel rims to accept the latest balloon tyres and improve ride comfort were fitted as standard. At the same time, the speedometer became part of the standard equipment. In April that year, the windscreen was modified with a slightly deeper opening top section and then in June or July new shock absorbers of Austin's own design replaced the earlier type and a magneto-type ignition system was introduced. All these early models had their headlamps mounted on the scuttle, and most had a black radiator shell, although some shells seem to have been painted in the body colour.

Although the four-seat Tourer remained central to the Austin Seven range in these early years, Austin recognised from the beginning that there was potential for a light Delivery Van derivative of their new economy car. The company produced its own design for such a vehicle but chose not to complicate production at the Longbridge works by building it there. Instead, it sub-contracted manufacture of the

Simple but charming... this was the 1923 Austin Seven Touring Car.

The folding top was simple to erect but its shape was not ideal for rear-seat passengers.

Delivery Vans to a Birmingham body builder called Startin. Production of these began about six months after the first Tourers left Longbridge. In the mean time, the Seven's potential as a competition car had been amply demonstrated, both by a works-prepared car and by one privately prepared by Gordon England, and so a natural choice for the next new derivative was a Sports model that joined the range in early 1924. A few months after that, there were some revisions for the Tourers.

In these early years, Austin were never afraid to explore the possibilities for their smallest model. Their own experiments embraced a Doctor's Coupé design, a Commercial Traveller's Car, and a Taxi Cab, although only the coupé was carried forward to production. The company also learned a good deal by making bare chassis available to independent coachbuilders – which was of course a common practice in the motor industry at the time – and seeing how well or otherwise the creations of these independents performed in the market. The success of models produced by Gordon England in particular (see Chapter 7) indicated the way forward for the factory-produced Sevens.

This was a period when the Seven gradually established itself as the standard for British economy cars, and by the end of 1925 Austin had a clear idea of where its appeal lay and how that appeal could be broadened to attract more sales. Some of the models that entered production between 1923 and 1925 remained available into the early months of 1926, but before Easter that year the entire range had been renewed in one way or another.

STARTIN, THE DELIVERY VAN BUILDERS

Thomas Startin's company was founded to build horse-drawn vehicles in 1840, and by the 1920s specialised in commercial bodywork for motor vehicles and was a motor agent as well. The company's premises were on the corner of Aston Road North and Holland Road, in the Nechells area of Birmingham that now has a B6 postcode. In later years, they specialised in hearses and extended-wheelbase limousines, selling their coachbuilding business in the late 1990s to the armoured-vehicle specialists S MacNeillie & Son of Walsall. The company now belongs to the Startin Group, which has multiple automotive businesses and car dealerships in the Midlands.

Tourer chassis were delivered from the Austin works at Longbridge to Startin for bodying as Delivery Vans. The Delivery Vans did not have their own factory letter codes, but were instead known by the code of the Tourer model on which they were based.

THE 1922 PROTOTYPES (MAY 1922)

The first three prototypes of the Seven were all Tourers, numbered XL1 to XL3. They were built in a screened-off area of the Austin works at Longbridge in May and June 1922, and were used to prove the soundness of the basic design.

These cars had a 696cc engine, a scuttle-mounted petrol tank, and a three-piece, lift-off bonnet. The second one was built with an open propshaft, which gave trouble and was dropped from the design. The bodies had ash frames and hand-beaten alloy panels, which was very much in the tradition of the day. They had two doors, two fixed front seats, and a rear bench seat.

The third prototype, XL3 (OK 3537) was judged to have the best transmission design and became the basis of the production cars. It was retained by Austin for many years but was presented to the Science Museum on loan in 1953. At some point before that, it had been incorrectly restored with running-boards that it did not have when first built, but it has since been returned to original condition and original colour.

Probably the earliest picture ever taken of an Austin Seven, this shows prototype XL-1 with Sir Herbert Austin at the wheel. The basic shape of the car was already there, although there were no running-boards.

XL3, the third prototype (Matthew Barker)

TYPE A TOURER, 1922-1923 (NOVEMBER 1922)

The first production Sevens were unsurprisingly known as Type A models and for public consumption were initially known by the description of Touring Car. They were very similar to the last of the 1922 prototypes, but incorporated minor improvements. The body was slightly longer and now featured running-boards, and the gear lever was slightly longer, too.

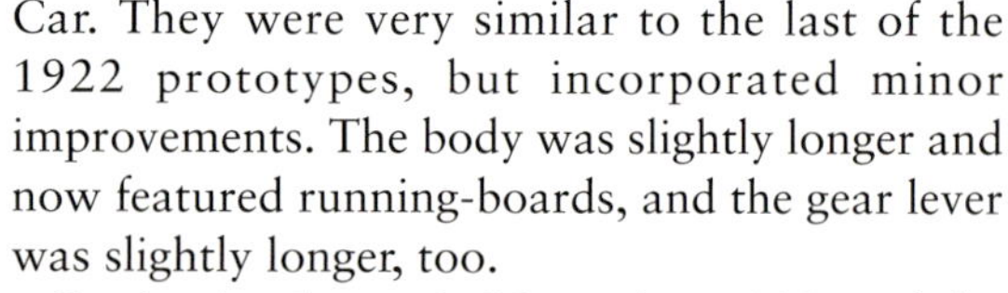

Production began in November 1922, and the Seven was introduced to the public at the Olympia Show in same month. The launch price was £225, but Austin quickly realised that this was too high and in December lowered it to £165 with the aim of appealing to motor cyclists who might be interested in changing to four wheels. The first public deliveries were made in January 1923, and production of the Type A Tourers continued until March, by which time 100 had been made.

The first 100 cars were numbered from A1-101, but the first two remained as chassis and the first body was fitted to car numbered A1-103. All of them had the original 696cc engine.

Production models added running-boards, as seen here. Clear in this picture are the early pram-type.

TYPE B CHUMMY TOURER, 1923-1924 (MARCH 1923)

The second iteration of the Seven Tourer was introduced in March 1923 and lasted until June 1924. Priced at the same £165 as the Type A, the car now had an enlarged 747cc engine.

These cars were popularly known as Chummy types, a name that was never officially used by Austin itself. "Chummy" was a familiar word meaning "friendly", which all four passengers needed to be in the confines of a Seven Tourer. It also helped to distinguish this type of Tourer from a two-seater with dickey seat, where the dickey seat passengers were physically separated from those in front by the car's bodywork.

This 1923 Chummy again has the early scalloped scuttle and pram-type folding hood. The early bonnet was a three-piece type that lifted off, the headlamps were mounted on the scuttle, and the radiator shell was finished in black. (Cars Down Under)

COUPÉ PROTOTYPES, 1923 (JULY 1923)

Austin looked at building a Doctor's Coupé in this period, but the idea did not go forward to production. Perhaps the company concluded that the market for such a model was covered well enough by independent specialists, or that it was too small to justify the necessary investment at Longbridge.

The Doctor's Coupé was a popular type in the 1920s, and its sales were obviously not confined solely to medical men. It was what would now be called a "three-box" design, with a projecting luggage boot behind the enclosed two-seater body. The name probably came from the fact that this configuration was ideal for a medical practitioner travelling on his own who wanted to keep his medical kit readily accessible but separate from the driving compartment; the separate boot did the job admirably.

The first prototype car was built in 1923 for Irene Waite, Sir Herbert Austin's daughter and the wife of Austin Director Arthur Waite. The car

This is a replica of the prototype Coupé that was built for Irene Waite, Herbert Austin's daughter. (Clive Barker).

Rear view of the first prototype Coupé replica. (Clive Barker).

was actually converted from a prototype Tourer that Mrs Waite was already using, probably with the aim of basing the new model on the Tourer with minimal alterations. It was a neat enough design and was originally fitted with Michelin easy-clean disc wheels, although these were later replaced with standard Austin wires. A change of registration number in July 1923 suggests a likely date for the conversion.

The second prototype was again built on the chassis of a pre-production Tourer, with an ash frame and aluminium panels. It was completed in 1924 and was lent to Earl Howe, a prominent racing driver who was also a friend of Arthur Waite. Perhaps he had seen Mrs Waite's car and had asked for a similar one for himself; there appear not to have been many differences between the two cars, although the 1924 car always had wire wheels and a black radiator shell instead of the nickel-plated one on the first car. This second car still survives, in preservation.

A third car was completed in March 1925, and it appears that Austin believed the Coupé might appeal to lady drivers. This was again a three-box design, now fitted with a luggage rack on the flat top of the boot. It was based on the contemporary Type C Tourer lower body with an aluminium-over-ash upper section that was covered in black Rexine. The body was later removed and stored at Longbridge, and in 1929 was mounted on a new chassis. In that guise, it still survives today.

TYPE B DELIVERY VAN, 1923-1924 (OCTOBER 1923)

The first of the Startin-bodied vans were based on the chassis of the Type B Tourer, which was introduced in March 1923. The earliest vans were built in October 1923 and were rated to carry a load of 2½ cwt (280 lb, 127kg). All would have had running-boards and the recently-enlarged 747cc engine. At £180 with the electric starter, the Delivery Van cost £10 more than a Chummy Tourer.

The Austin-designed van body had an ash framework with aluminium panelling, and the bonnet, scuttle, bulkhead and doors were those of the parent Type B Tourer. The radiator shell, headlamps, wheels, mudguards and running boards were always black, and the vans were sold with a primer finish unless painted to suit the customer. Austin would not supply special colours but only those it used on its production models.

There were no side windows for the cab

The Delivery Van was designed by Austin but built by Startin. Its shape was most attractive, although there was minimal weather protection for the driver.

area and the open area above the half-height doors had a distinctive C-shape at the rear. Attached to the cant rail above each door was a rolled-up sidescreen that could be deployed to provide a degree of weather protection for both the driver and passenger. The doors had no exterior handles. The cab was furnished with a single bench seat, which was always trimmed in black Rexine, and there was a full-height bulkhead with a small rectangular window between the driving compartment and the load area behind. The spare wheel was carried within the body, mounted to this bulkhead.

The roof was at its highest in the middle, and sloped downwards at both the front and rear. There were twin rear doors, each of which had an oval window, and the headlamps were mounted on the scuttle. These models were in production for just over a year, but there is no reliable indication of how many were made.

The space in the body was tall and quite narrow, and the Delivery Van was rated to carry 2½ cwt (280 lb/127kg). A shrewd viewer of this catalogue illustration might have wondered where the spare wheel was kept…

COMMERCIAL TRAVELLER'S CAR, 1923 (LATE 1923)

Austin built two prototypes of a Commercial Traveller's Car in late 1923, which was clearly related to their plans for light commercial derivatives of the Seven that had already borne fruit with the Delivery Van built by Startins.

These two prototypes were based on the Type B Tourer of the time, with an additional body structure at the rear that provided a van-like appearance and contained shelves for the storage of samples. The second car had a lower roof line than the first, and Austin advertised its availability in *The Light Car and Cyclecar* of 26 October 1923. *The Autocar* also reported on the planned new model, and a price of £170 was quoted, but in practice no production followed.

October 26, 1923 THE LIGHT CAR AND CYCLECAR 9

For the "Commercial"

The "Austin Seven" is now presented in ideal form for the commercial traveller. It has 10½ cubic feet space for carrying samples up to 2½ cwt. The speed and reliability of this car are well-known, and by its use the traveller can, while keeping fresh and clean, explore new districts inaccessible by railway, taking his goods with him from factory to the customer's door.

Write for descriptive folder.

THE AUSTIN MOTOR CO., LIMITED,
Longbridge — Near BIRMINGHAM.
London: 479-483, Oxford Street, W.1 (near Marble Arch).

Features:

Carries 2½ cwt.
4-cylinder engine.
Water-cooled.
Detachable head.
Automatic lubrication
Three-speed gearbox.
Bevel drive.
Differential.
Brakes on all wheels.
Electric lighting and horn.

The Austin Seven

Just two prototypes of the Commercial Traveller's Car were built, although the model was advertised for sale in this press advertisement.

50MPH SPORTS, 1924-1926 (MARCH 1924)

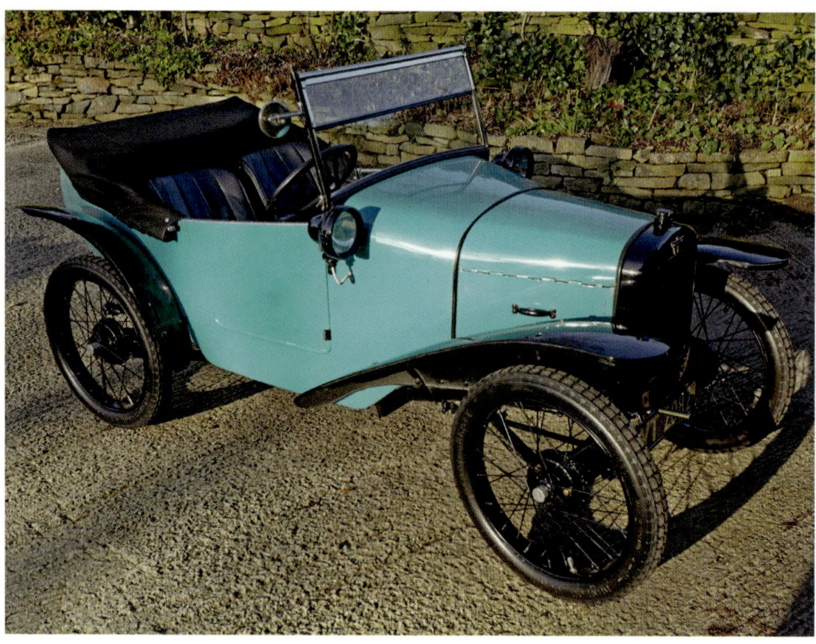

The first Longbridge-built sports model was the 50mph type in 1924. The pointed tail and flared wings were typical sporting design cues of the time. A straight-sided scuttle had replaced the scalloped type by this time. (Nick Turley)

The first Sports version of the Seven that Austin built themselves was called the 50mph Sports and made its debut in March 1924 at Car Number A1-3126. In theory, even a standard Seven Tourer could reach 50mph, but much depended on how many passengers it was carrying. The point of the 50mph Sports was that it could generally be relied upon to achieve that speed; with only two seats, its all-up weight was obviously lower, and taller final drive gearing of 4.4:1 helped as well. For a small economy car, the name was a quite shrewd piece of marketing. Even so, the December 1924 advertisement that spoke of "a whirlwind of dynamic power called forth by the movement of a finger" deserves a special prize for hyperbole.

The chassis was essentially a standard Seven type, running on 26in wheels with skinny 3in tyres, but its steering column was more steeply raked at an angle of 41 degrees so that the body could have a lower dash and could generally appear more sporting. The body consisted of aluminium panels on an ash frame, and was designed around several "fast-car" visual cues of the day. It was a two-seater with a long tapering tail that had a rounded end, there were no running-boards, and the skimpy steel wings were very Gallic in inspiration, designed to look aerodynamic and mounted so that their undersides were visible to someone standing next to the car. The doors had cut-down tops to allow young bloods to rest an elbow nonchalantly while driving, and had no external handles, and the top section of the windscreen could be removed to reduce wind resistance if the owner wanted to use the car for speed events.

The folding hood could be removed altogether, too, but when erected was a most ungainly piece of work. The spare wheel was normally carried out of sight within the long tail, but an Austin works modification was to mount it on top of the rear panel. Interior trim was rather spartan, but that was what sporting drivers expected and wanted.

The 50mph Sports was built until early 1926, and the general consensus is that around 300 were built. Its showroom price was £175 in the beginning, but this was lowered to £170 in October 1924. By September 1926, what must have been old-stock models were on offer at £159. The last of the 50mph Sports were fitted with full touring wings and running boards.

The last of the 50mph Sports had touring wings and running boards.

TYPE C CHUMMY TOURERS, 1924-1926 (JUNE 1924)

The Tourer was revised yet again in June 1924, becoming a Type C. Arguably, it was a little less "chummy" than before because the body had been lengthened by 2½ in – but the customers would not have complained and of course the familiar epithet remained in use. A further benefit of the extra length was wider doors with sloping rear edges that improved access to the rear seats, and the folding hood was also modified with a squarer shape at the rear that gave more headroom.

The scuttle now had flat sides and the bonnet was modified to suit. The radiator shell and scuttle-mounted headlamps were finished in black as standard, and there was just one colour choice available: Kingfisher Blue with Black wings. Wings and running-boards were also changed from the Type B pattern early in production (at chassis number A1-4771), but the only other major change during the model's production life was made in February 1925, when a speedometer was made standard and the tyre width was increased from 3in to 3½in.

Sevens were selling strongly enough by summer 1924 for the Type C to be introduced at the further reduced price of £155 – £10 or 6% less than its Type B predecessor. Austin passed on the unit savings to customers as increasing volumes allowed, lowering the price to £149 in September 1925. The last of these models left the assembly lines in March 1926.

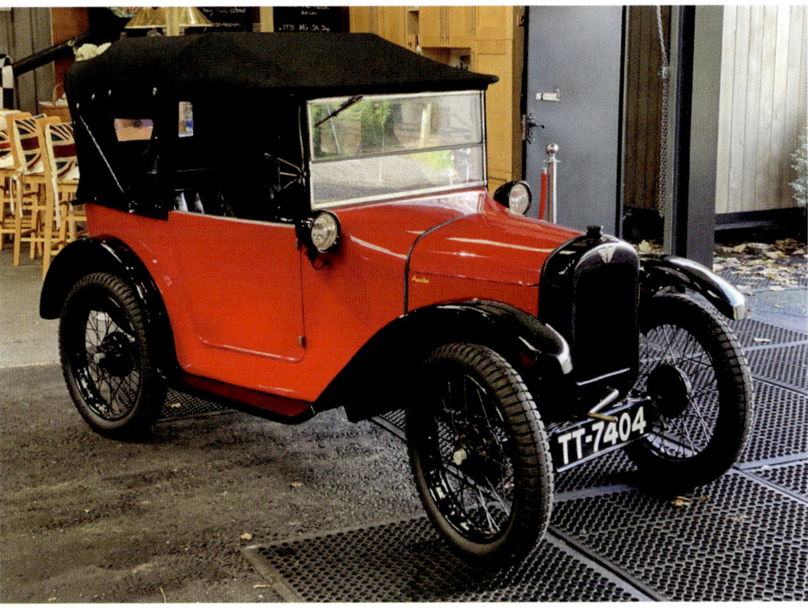

The Type C Tourer, also known as an AC, still had the pram-type hood. This well-known example was new in July 1925. (Robin Lawton)

TYPE C DELIVERY VAN, 1924-1926 (AUGUST 1924 APPROX)

A few months after the Type C Tourer with its multiple improvements replaced the Type B Tourer in June 1924, the Startin-bodied van switched to the new front end and flat-sided scuttle. Otherwise, the body remained largely unchanged from that of the earlier Startin van, but the bulkhead behind the cab now had a small window. In other respects they shared their specification with the parent Tourer, having the same three-piece bonnet with plain sides, and the same horizontally split opening windscreen.

These revised Delivery Vans were probably available from late summer 1924, and were built for just under two years. The Type C Tourer was discontinued in March 1926 when the further revised Type D Tourer was introduced, and the Startin vans followed suit. Once again, there is unfortunately no reliable evidence of production quantities, although the likelihood is that somewhere between 200 and 300 were built in each full year of their availability.

By the time of this Type C Delivery Van in 1924 the scuttle was no longer scalloped.

COUPÉ 1925-1926 (JANUARY 1925)

Following the earlier prototypes, the Company launched a coupé in January 1925 following the same general 3-box style, but with significant detail differences. Based on the Type-C tourer body, the doors were fitted with three hinges and a non-removeable window frame, the rear side windows were deleted, and the boot was smaller and more angular with provision for carrying extra luggage on a rack affixed to the top. Produced only in small numbers, the last were sold in early 1926, although possibly of late 1925 manufacture.

The Coupé was produced only in small numbers. This illustration shows a 1925 car.

The 1925 Coupé was priced at £165, with laminated glass available at twelve guineas extra.

TAXI PROTOTYPES, 1925 (JANUARY 1925)

The single-passenger Taxi was a good idea in theory, but did not work so well in practice. This version has a sliding rear window with what looks like "purdah" (privacy) glass and a taximeter is mounted to the far side of the windscreen frame.

Austin identified a potential market for a single-passenger taxi that would be suited for use in large towns and cities, where larger conventional taxis (of which the Austin company was already making many) were relatively expensive and unnecessary for the single business person wishing to hire transport.

The first prototype was completed in January 1925 and was based on the lower body of the contemporary Type C Tourer, fitted with a fabric-covered roof section. The space beside the driver was allocated to luggage in the traditional British taxi fashion, and a single seat was fitted transversely in the rear, facing the kerb. Passenger access was through the single kerb side door, and a fixed screen divided driver from passenger. The doors had three hinges instead of the usual two, presumably to help them withstand heavy use, and apertures above them remained permanently open, with no weather protection for the driver.

A dozen examples of the Austin Seven Taxi were completed and went on extended trials in London, and one vehicle (without the sliding rear side windows of the prototype) was displayed at the Commercial Motor Show at Olympia in October 1925. However, the London trial revealed that passengers actually disliked travelling alone, and so the cars were recalled to Longbridge and converted into standard Tourers.

This example of the Taxi was exhibited at the Commercial Motor Show in October 1925, but has neither the sliding rear window nor a taximeter.

Identification, 1923-1925

Austin Sevens in this period are usually identified by their Car Number, which is shown on the service plate. This is a zinc disc that is screwed to the left-hand door pillar.

Car Numbers consist of a sequence prefix (eg A2) followed by a four-digit serial number between 101 and 9999. Car Numbers and Chassis Numbers matched in this period, so that Car Number A2-700 had Chassis Number 10700. Engine Numbers had a separate and unrelated sequence.

The sequence prefixes relevant to the 1922-1925 period are: A1, commencing March 1923 A2, May 1925

The first production car was numbered A1-101 in March 1923. It is not clear how cars built before March 1923 were numbered.

No build records for cars of this period survive.

Production totals, 1922-1925

Below are the generally accepted annual production figures for the Austin Seven.

1922	178
1923	2409
1924	4800
1925	8024

Individual type totals are not available, except as noted in the text.

Technical Specifications, 1923-1925

Engine: Four-cylinder side-valve

Capacity: 1922-1923: 696ccc; 1923-1925: 747.5ccc

Bore x stroke: 1922-1923: 54mm x 76mm ; 1923-1925: 56mm x 76mm

Induction: 1922-1923: Zenith type 22FE carburettor; 1923-1925: Zenith type 22FZ carburettor (bronze body)

Power: 696cc: 10bhp at 2400rpm; 747cc: 10.5bhp at 2400rpm

Gearbox: Three-speed with reverse. 3.20:1, 1.80:1, 1.00:1; reverse 4.28:1

Axle ratio: Standard 5.5:1 (with 696cc engine), 4.9:1 (with 747cc engine), Sports 4.4:1, Milk Delivery Car 5.625:1

Brakes: Drums all round, 6in x 1in. Footbrake operated rear pair and handbrake operated front pair

Steering: Worm and wheel type

Front suspension: Beam axle with transverse leaf spring and radius arms

Rear suspension: Beam axle with quarter-elliptic leaf springs

Wheels and tyres: Wire spoked wheels with 26in diameter; 1922-1923 rims for beaded-edge tyres. Dunlop Cord tyres fitted to first prototype, Dunlop Magnum Cord tyres to the third. 1922-1923 – 26in x 3in tyres. Cost option From early 1924 – 26in x 3½ in balloon tyres; standard from Feb 1925

Length: First prototype – 105in/2667mm, Third prototype – 104in/2641mm, 1922-1924 – 106in/2692mm,

Wheelbase: 75in/1905mm

Width: 46in/1168mm

Front Track: 40in/1016mm

Rear Track: 43in/1092mm

Weight: First prototype – 672 lb/305kg, Third prototype – 728 lb/330kg 1922-1924 – 785 lb/355kg, Delivery Van (gross weight) – 896 lb/406kg,

MAJOR EXPANSION, 1926-1931

Up to the end of 1925, the Austin Seven range had been centred on the Tourer model, which had also formed the basis for a Delivery Van and, from 1925, a Sports Two-seater and Coupé. In the mean time, the Seven had become the basis for competition models that had attracted considerable attention, while bare chassis sold to independent specialists had been bodied in a variety of ways. From early in 1926, there was a noticeable step-change in Austin's approach to its smallest model, as new variants began to appear. The most important of them in the longer term was undoubtedly a Saloon. The development of the range was greatly helped by the major production facility changes engineered by Works Director, Charles Englebach.

This chapter therefore looks at the new models that were introduced between early 1926 and the next major change in Austin Seven production, which was the introduction of a longer wheelbase in summer 1931. Of the earlier models, only the Type C Tourer or Chummy remained into production during the early months of 1926.

The usual round of adjustments and improvements began almost as soon as the first of these models entered production. Two important changes were made in the early autumn as the 1927 models were about to come on-stream, as all models were given deeper side frames in August 1926 and 7in brake drums in place of the original 6in size from September. August also brought heavier road springs for the Saloon models, and these were fitted as standard to all Sevens destined for export.

One of the more amusing episodes in Austin Seven history began in September 1926, when the headlamps were moved from the scuttle to the front wings (and a four-piece bonnet replaced the earlier three-piece type). The Hampshire Police then objected that they were not as close to the edges of the car as the law required and, instead of redesigning the mounting brackets, Austin simply moved the lights back to their original position in January 1927. The company

For a brief interlude in 1926-1927, headlamps were moved to the wings from their original position on the scuttle; they then moved back to the scuttle again.

also offered a conversion kit that enabled owners with wing-mounted headlamps to relocate them on the scuttle. Once the question over headlamp positions had been satisfactorily resolved, Austin reverted to their original intention and from August 1928, with the introduction of the larger R47 headlamps, the lamps were moved to positions on the front wings, with redesigned mounting brackets that complied with legal requirements.

Major changes included the rearward extension of the frame side-members in December 1927, to give better support to the body, and a change to coil ignition in September 1928. August 1928 had brought redesigned wings and a new nickel-finish radiator shell; a script Austin name was added to the radiator itself in May 1929. The engine gained larger bearings in October 1929, and the position of the tank filler was changed a month later.

A further important visual change was made in June 1930, when the scuttle was made shorter (and the bonnet correspondingly longer), which had the effect of making the car look longer. This arrangement was further adjusted in February 1931 when the scuttle was lengthened slightly, and the bonnet again modified to suit. From July 1930, the front and rear brakes were coupled together, so that the footbrake pedal and handbrake lever both acted on all four wheels.

There were multiple new models in this period, which also saw a general move away from fabric-panelled bodies and towards metal-panelled types. Saloons began with the Types R and RF in April 1926 and progressed through the RK (September 1928) to the RL and RG (May 1930), and then to the RM and RH (January 1931). Tourers began with the Type AD, which was followed in September 1929 by the Type AE and in June 1930 by the Type AF.

Austin took production of the Delivery Vans in-house from June 1930 and began with the Type VD, and that September added another light commercial called the Milk Delivery Car or Type VB. There were small numbers of Coupé bodies between 1928 and 1930, and a two-seat Tourer joined the ranks in January 1929, progressing from Type P to Type PA, to Type PB in June 1930 and Type PC in 1931. Lastly, the sporting fraternity was offered special models: the Super Sports from July 1928 and the legendary Ulster or EA Sports from April 1930.

TYPE D/AD TOURER, 1926-1929 (MARCH 1926)

Austin's constant search for more room within the Seven's body led to another redesign of the Tourer, which appeared in March 1926 as the Type D (and was later known as the AD). The redesign brought additional width, greater length, and extra knee room, and there was even room to store the sidescreens at the rear as well.

From the outside, the Type D could be recognised by a new windscreen with a lower edge that was curved to match the profile of the scuttle. The hood, too, was more angular than on earlier Tourers to give more room for the rear-seat passengers. The sidescreens no longer had flaps to give access to the interior door releases because there were now proper outside door handles. Initially, these were mounted horizontally in the conventional manner, but from September 1928 they were repositioned vertically, with the open ends pointing downwards. The radiator shell and headlamps were still finished in black.

Some important changes were made during the production run of these models. The first few cars had 6in brakes but 7in brakes were soon standardised. From August 1926, the chassis gained stronger side rails, and a month later came not only larger brake drums but the very visible alteration of headlamps mounted on the wings instead of on the scuttle. This sequence of changes

This early Type D Tourer still has the headlamps on the scuttle. The folding top had been redesigned to give more headroom for rear-seat passengers.

Headlamps were still on the scuttle by the time of this June 1928 Type AD Tourer. (Simon Clay)

ended in October 1926 with the standardisation of a vacuum-operated windscreen wiper and a four-piece bonnet that improved engine access over the earlier three-piece type.

Until August 1928, the AD Tourers once again carried their headlamps mounted on the sides of the scuttle, then the lamps went back to the wings and thereafter stayed there. There was another change in August 1928, when the black-painted radiator shell was replaced by a black nickel-plated type.

This was the most numerous Seven body of its time, and was introduced at chassis number 17074. Austin continued to drive down showroom prices. Initially £149 like the Type C Tourers that had preceded them, the Type D models dropped to £145 in September 1926 and to £135 in August 1927. In August 1928 the price came down again to £125 but by January 1929 it was back up at £130. Triplex safety glass was available from the beginning and, of course, cost extra. The Type D Tourer remained in production until September 1929.

TYPE R SALOON, 1926-1928 (APRIL 1926)

The first Longbridge-built Austin Seven Saloon was the Type R, which was introduced in April 1926 and remained in production until the late autumn of 1928. In the intervening two and a half years, an estimated 5000 examples were built, and the price was progressively reduced. What was initially known as the Special Saloon cost £168 in its most expensive form (with Triplex safety glass) or £150 in standard form on its introduction. By September 1928, the price had dropped to £135.

The Saloon body had a roof partly covered in rexine, ending just short of the rear, and aluminium panels over its ash frame. There were four equal-sized side windows with sliding glass, plus a split windscreen to provide ventilation.All Type Rs were fitted with vacuum windscreen wipers. The two doors were hinged at the rear and although early cars had the three-piece bonnet, the new four-piece centre-hinged type became standard from September 1926.

All the early Type R Saloons had scuttle-mounted headlamps, but from September 1926 the lamps were mounted on brackets on the front wings. As explained above, they went back to the scuttle from January 1927 and stayed there until sanity prevailed and they could return to the wings in August 1928. Early Type R Saloons were not fitted with ventilators in the scuttle sides.

The chassis and mechanical specification of these cars generally followed mainstream developments on the Seven, so that (for example), they gained deeper chassis side-members in August 1926 and switched from 6in brake drums to a 7in size in September that year. Of note is that the body side panel behind the doors tended to split on early models, and from December 1927 Austin cured this problem with a rearward chassis extension that was also made available as a service modification.

The Type R was replaced by the Type RK in September 1928, but continued in production alongside the new model into November. The last cars, from around August 1928 were quite different to the earlier cars, showing features of the RK. They had a taller nickel-plated radiator shell; scuttle ventilators as standard, the headlamps were back on the wings, there was a flat steering wheel, side pockets in the dashboard, no edge beading around the doors, a larger radius on the door trailing edge, a 'clasp' join in the bodywork above the rear wheelarch and the rexine roof covering extended all the way back. Most of these late cars were fitted with new coil engine, although some came with the magneto type.

The Type R with equal-sized front and rear side windows was Austin's first Seven Saloon.

The last Type R saloons, from August 1928, gained some features from the replacement RK model, including a larger radius on the door trailing edge and a 'clasp' join in the bodywork by the rear wheelarch.

TYPE D/AD DELIVERY VAN, 1926-1930 (JUNE 1926)

The van bodies built by Startins were revised a few months after the Type D (later AD) four-seat Tourers took over from the Type C Tourer in March 1926. The overall shape nevertheless remained unchanged, and these vans continued to have a horizontally split windscreen with an opening upper section. One obvious change was associated with the cab doors, which now had an angled trailing edge as well as external handles.

Some changes were made in the first autumn of production. The first examples of the Type D van in June 1926 had their headlamps mounted on the scuttle like their predecessors, but from September these were relocated on the front wings. A four-piece bonnet replaced the original three-piece type in October, and the headlamps probably changed position again twice over the next 15 months, as they did on the parent Type D Tourer.

Over the first year or so of production, the price was reduced twice, probably because of competition from the Gordon England vans. These were £5 more expensive than the Startin van, but Gordon England was more amenable to bespoke variations, and also had the benefit of a fully-enclosed driving compartment. Once again, total production numbers are unknown, although it is clear that the company built 326 of them during 1928.

From some time in late 1929, the Startin vans were built on the Type AE Tourer chassis, although the Type AD designation remained in use. The AE-based vans used that model's bulkhead and scuttle with its plated letter-box ventilator on the kerb side, and their chassis were fitted with stronger road springs than those of the parent Tourer. Production ended in June 1930.

If annual volumes were fairly constant, the total of 326 vans built in 1928 suggests that there would have been somewhere between 1200 and 1500 based on the Type D and Type AE Tourer chassis.

The angled trailing edge of the door and exterior door handles help to identify these two 1927 Delivery Vans as Type D models, built by Startins. (far right, Clive Barker)

EXPERIMENTAL PICK-UP, 1929

Various features of this pick-up suggest a 1929 build date, but there is no hard information about it.

Very little is known about a pick-up derivative of the Seven that was probably built at Longbridge some time around the summer of 1929. It had C-shaped side window apertures similar to those on the Startin vans but the spare wheel was carried outside the body on the passenger's side, where there was of course no door. A picture shows a three-piece bonnet but with wing-mounted headlamps, and in tandem these features suggest a build date just before wing-mounted lamps were introduced and just as the three-piece bonnet was about to be replaced by the four-piece type. The pick-up might possibly have been inspired by the "ute" (utility) trucks being built on Seven chassis in Australia, but it was not pursued at Longbridge.

TYPE RF SALOON, 1926-1930 (SEPTEMBER 1926)

The Type RF was the fabric-panelled alternative to the Type R Saloon, and it is not hard to see how the identifying initials were derived. It was introduced in September or October 1926, some six months after the metal-panelled car, and consistently out-sold it by a large margin for the rest of the decade while fabric bodies remained fashionable. Although the first signs that buyers were turning away from fabric-bodied Saloons were already visible, Austin decided to replace the Type RF with a new fabric-bodied model when it went out of production around summer 1930.

This early RF Saloon has its headlamps mounted on the scuttle.

Although the surviving photograph of a prototype fabric-bodied Saloon shows a body with the equal-sized side windows of the Type R metal-panelled Saloon, the production models had the longer front-hinged doors and fixed rear side windows associated with the RK Saloon (see below). The body frame was made of ash wood, which was then padded and covered with canvas, and with Rexine on the roof. The RF was nevertheless not entirely fabric-panelled. The lower door panels still had aluminium skins and there was aluminium across the scuttle to provide support for the fabric outer skin.

Early RF models had scuttle-mounted headlamps, apparently escaping the revisions that affected the contemporary metal-panelled Saloons in 1926-1927. None of them had scuttle ventilators. Later models nevertheless had both wing-mounted headlamps and plated scuttle ventilators.

From September 1928, what was generally called the Austin Seven Fabric Saloon was priced at £150 or £168 with the addition of Triplex safety glass, which turned it into a Special Model. A sliding sunroof could be had at extra cost, as on the contemporary metal-bodied Seven Saloon. As Bryan Purves has noted, the 100,000th Austin Seven, which was completed in July 1929, was a Fabric Saloon with the long roof peak and plated scuttle ventilators.

By the time the last examples of the RF were built in October 1930, the price of the Fabric Saloon had dropped to the same as that of its metal-panelled contemporary – £140 or £145 with sliding roof.

The fabric-bodied RF saloons developed in line with the contemporary Type R Saloon. This later 1928 Type RF Saloon has wing-nounted headlamps and scuttle venitlators. (Matthew Barker)

SUPER SPORTS, 1928-1930 (JULY 1928)

The next new iteration of the sporting Seven was more deliberately aimed at the owner who planned to use the car for competition work. The first car was developed in 1927, shipped to Australia to Captain Arthur Waite (Austin's son-in-law) and was raced successfully in the 1928 Australian Grand Prix. Concurrent with Waite's car, a further two were built, officially designated as Super Sports, being debuted at Shelsley Walsh in July 1928. Public availability was announced after that event, at a price of £225 – a figure that made it very expensive against the £150 then being asked for an Austin Seven saloon.

The key ingredient in the Super Sports was an engine that had been extensively modified from standard. Still with 747cc, it had a counterbalanced crankshaft, balanced pistons and conrods, and stronger valve springs; and on most cars, to this was added a gear-driven Cozette supercharger mounted on the exhaust side and operating at 6psi. There was also a water pump to deal with the increased heat generated by the more heavily-stressed engine.

Production engines were also capable of revving to nearly 7000rpm, and if the claimed maximum output of 27bhp at 4500rpm sounds feeble by modern standards, it is important to remember that the standard 747cc engine at that time was delivering just 13bhp. The supercharged engine thus brought a power increase of more than 100%!

As usual, the body was panelled with aluminium over an ash frame, but in this case it had no doors at all and deep U-shaped cutaways on either side of the cockpit served to make climbing in and out easier for the occupants. There was an upswept scuttle, a standard Chummy bonnet and black painted radiator cowl. The front wings terminated in a short step that also helped entry and exit, and there were no running-boards. However, as the exhaust ran on the outside of the bodywork next to the passenger, an additional step was provided on that side. The tail was pointed but its profile was different from that of the earlier Sports models, and the spare wheel was carried within it under a detachable cover panel.

On cars sold to the public, a three-speed gearbox with standard ratios was offered, together with the same 4.4:1 axle ratio that had featured on earlier Sports models. However,

Considerably enhanced with the aid of an airbrush, this photograph nevertheless gives a good idea of the way the supercharged 1928 Super Sports looked.

there was an optional axle ratio of 5.66:1 as well, which maximised acceleration at some cost to top speed. The cockpit was arranged in suitably sporting fashion, with two separate seats, the one on the passenger's side mounted slightly further back than the driver's seat to suit the duties of a racing mechanic or co-driver. The steering column was also raked at 37½ degrees, a steeper angle than on earlier Sports models.

Some changes were made in 1929, when the co-driver's seat was repositioned alongside the driver's seat and standard touring wings were fitted. The suspension was also lowered by a whole 3 inches, by fitting reverse-camber springs with dropped front radius arms and a drop-centre front axle. Production was brought to an end in April 1930.

Five Super Sports "works" cars were built in 1927-1928, and these were even more highly tuned to deliver more than 30bhp and a top speed of more than 80mph. The engines of course had counterbalanced crankshafts, as well as changes to the valve gear and cast aluminium sumps. A close-ratio gearbox was fitted, and several different axle ratios were used. Austin entered these cars in the 1929 Ulster TT race, where they put up a magnificent performance (even though they were denied a win) and this event led ultimately to the legendary Type EA or Ulster model.

TYPE RK SALOON, 1928-1930 (SEPTEMBER 1928)

A major body redesign created the Type RK Saloon that was introduced in September 1928. The panels were once again in aluminium, but the major difference lay in the much longer doors and correspondingly shorter rear side windows – which now had fixed panes. The doors were of course now hinged on the A-posts and had a large cutaway at the rear to fit around the forward edge of the wheelarch. A further characteristic of these bodies was a sizeable "peak" over the one-piece windscreen, a feature that was actually reduced in size in December 1928, just a few months after production began.

The RK Saloon looked very different from the Type R Saloon, with a long door window and a short rear side window.

The RK Saloons had a long scuttle and a four-piece bonnet. On the earliest examples, the headlamps were mounted on the scuttle but of course soon moved to the wings. The bodies were typically turned out with a two-tone finish, the darker colour covering the roof and window area. They could be ordered with a sliding sunroof, when Austin charged an additional £5 over the £135 for the standard car, and a folding luggage carrier at the rear was a further optional feature.

Dickon Armstrong's beautiful 1929 RK Saloon, Primrose, has an original Pytchley sunroof.

The RK model evolved during its production, and by July 1929 two different types of front wings were being used on production cars, no doubt partly to use up stocks of older types. In addition to the two sizes of peak above the windscreen, there were two different types of windscreen, one deeper than the other. Triplex glass had become standard by this stage, and the price had increased to £140, again with an extra £5 needed to add the optional sliding roof.

Production of the RK continued until July 1930, by which time the replacement Type RL was already in production.

A rear three-quarter view of a 1929 RK Saloon. (Clive Barker)

TYPE B/BA COUPÉ, 1928-1930 (OCTOBER 1928)

The first completely new model after the Seven's headlamps had moved permanently to the front wings was a Coupé, which was introduced in October 1928. Originally known as the Type B, the BA designation was used to bring it into line with the other two-character references of the time.

Austin's original thoughts about a three-box Doctor's Coupé body were abandoned after 1925, and when the idea of a Coupé was revived three years later it had been re-imagined as what might now be called a two-door saloon, with two proper seats in the front and a small bench/shelf for luggage or small, willing children behind. To provide the space, the passenger compartment now reached the tail of

A beautifully preserved example of the Type B Coupé, in this case first registered in June 1930. (Clive Barker)

the car and there was no separate "boot".

The body was panelled in aluminium, with a fabric covering above the waistline, and the rear section of each door window could be slid open. All cars seem to have had a long scuttle.

Production continued until Autumn 1930, the last car being despatched in October, but proabably having been built some time before. A total of 533 Coupés appears to have been built in about two years.

This angle shows the neat rear of the Coupé. The body was panelled in aluminium whith fabric covering above the waistline. (Clive Barker)

TYPE P/PA TWO-SEATER, 1929-1930 (JANUARY 1929)

From the start of 1929, Austin added another new body variant to the Seven range in the shape of a Two-seater. It was called nothing more exciting than that, although other makers might perhaps have called it a two-seat Tourer or something similar. It was not intended as another sporting model despite its raked steering column, but as an alternative to the four-seat Tourer models.

The first of the Two-seater Sevens was given the Type P designation. To allow low lines, the steering column was more steeply raked than on other models, and the seats were also mounted on low frames.

The aluminium body was designed with a fashionable "boat-tail" and the spare wheel was carried flat within it. The top panel of the tail was hinged to give access, but this was impractical when the hood was folded and so access was also possible from inside the passenger compartment. These early Two-seaters had a long scuttle, a divided windscreen, and detachable side screens. Their doors were front-hinged and were shaped to fit around the rear wheel arch in the same way as on the Saloons of the time. A production figure of 100 is generally accepted.

Wide doors, a distinctive tail, and a long scuttle characterised the 1929 Type P Two-seater model.

TYPE AE TOURER, 1929-1930 (SEPTEMBER 1929)

Although the Type AE Tourer was superficially similar to the Type AD that preceded it, there were many differences. Perhaps most obvious here are the absence of beading around the doors, the bright-finish radiator surround, and the plated ventilators on the scuttle. By this time, wing-mounted headlamps were standard. (Simon Clay)

The next version of the Seven Tourer was almost certainly introduced in September 1929, at chassis number 96600. (Note, though, that some commentators have claimed an earlier date of introduction that year.) The first examples were priced at £130.

The Type AE once again provided extra body space while retaining the original chassis dimensions. This time the body was another two inches longer and 2½ in wider, while the roof line sloped upwards to give more headroom.

There had also been a redesign of the scuttle so that the petrol tank could be better located, and this was accompanied by ventilators on the sides of the scuttle itself and by a raised bonnet line. The wing profile was curved and a Triplex safety-glass windscreen was now standard. Although the first examples of the AE had nickel-plated radiator shells, from October 1929 chromed shells became standard. The canvas hood was also made easier to use with spring clips instead of the earlier fixing straps. There were changes inside, too, where the speedometer was relocated nearer the centre of the dash and a cubby cut-out was provided on either side.

Production of the Type AE Tourer probably continued until mid-1930, although the exact date has not been firmly established.

TYPE EA "ULSTER" SPORTS, 1930-1932 (APRIL 1930)

This nicely original supercharged EA Sports model belongs to Dr James Anderson.

During 1929, Austin built a single prototype, similar to the Super Sports with an aluminium-panelled body that had a pointed tail, non-staggered seating, cycle wings and an external exhaust on the passenger's side. The headlamps were mounted high up on the wing stays; the screen itself folded flat. The hood appears to have been very basic. The chassis was a production type fitted with a drop-centre front axle, flattened road springs, and the usual raked steering column.

This was the prototype for the Type EA Sports model which replaced the Super Sports. The first production examples of the car that would later become known as the Ulster were built in April 1930, although Ulster was never its official name. It came instead from enthusiastic owners and was applied from around August 1931 in honour of Austin successes in the 1929 and 1930 TT races that had been held in Ulster.

The body style echoed designs on earlier Austin Seven Sports models, and the panelwork was once again made of aluminium although the floorpan was steel. The pointed tail was similar to that of the Super Sports, but with less rearward taper at the top and with a smaller cover for the spare wheel which was mounted

This rear overhead view of the same car shows its pointed tail.

GH 23 is seen at Brooklands (left), when new in 1930, and today (above). The car remains in very original condition and belongs to Graham Beckett.

vertically behind the passenger compartment. There were no doors, and once again a cutout – more of a shallow V-shape in this instance – provided the necessary access. The exhaust was again routed along the passenger's side of the body and always ended in a fishtail.

The windscreen had no top rail and folded flat onto the bonnet, and there was a pram-type hood that folded down behind the seats and could be encased in its own cover, but no sidescreens were provided. The steel side panels of the long bonnet each had a row of louvres, and the front wings were braced by a tie bar that ran ahead of the radiator; headlamps were nevertheless bolted to the wings and not to the tie bar. There was a full set of wings and running-boards, modified from the type fitted to contemporary Tourers.

The Type EA Sports model could be had with its engine either tuned or supercharged. Here it is with screen lowered and hood removed; the distinctive external exhaust was of course on the other side of the car.

This artwork shows it with screen up and hood fitted – in touring trim.

Like the later Super Sports models, these were lowered by 3 inches. They had a drop-centre front axle beam, special radius rod ends, cranked steering arms, and a track rod to suit, and the transverse leaf spring at the front had a reversed camber and was bound with cord to improve stability.

The Ulster could be had from the start of production with either a tuned 747cc engine that had 24bhp at 5000rpm and delivered 60-65mph or a supercharged type that gave the car a top speed of about 77mph. As the Ulster was deliberately designed to work as either a road or a track car, there were performance options for those who wanted them. Competition gearsets were available and from 1931 there was also a a stronger cylinder block with ten studs and a high-compression 7:1 cylinder head that offered better cooling as well.

The Ulster in standard form cost £185, and the supercharged version cost the same £225 as the earlier Super Sports model. About 300 examples of all types are thought to have been built before production came to an end in January 1932.

TYPE RL SALOON, 1930-1931 (MAY 1930)

May 1930 brought new Saloon models of the Austin Seven, the metal-bodied Type RL and the related fabric-bodied Type RG (see below). The familiar "top hat" shape was still in place but the RL models had an important difference from their RK predecessors: their panels were now made of steel rather than aluminium. Production ended in February 1931 (but note that for a long time the dates of RL production were considered to be March 1930 to October 1931).

There was more curvature to the rear of the roof than on earlier models, although the Rexine covering remained a feature and it was still possible to order a sliding roof at extra cost. This was manufactured by Pytchley, and the cars that had it were sometimes described as Sunshine Saloons. On the solid-roof bodies, a roof ventilator or "smoker's vent" could be ordered. All versions had a straight-bottomed windscreen, but of course the design evolved in the usual way during production.

The RL Saloons had a longer, 27½-inch bonnet than their predecessors, without louvres (these arrived in September 1930), and this was matched to a tall, 6-inch scuttle. Instruments located in the centre of the dashboard and a fabric rear window blind were other features of the RL Saloons. On the mechanical side, they gained coupled brakes.

The RL Saloon cost £130, or £135 with the addition of the Pytchley sliding roof. De Luxe models were available with a two-colour finish.

The Type RL Saloon was a well-resolved design, with a gently curved tail panel. This is an early example, with neither scuttle vents nor bonnet louvres.

This later RL Saloon has the scuttle vents but the artist has omitted the bonnet louvres normally associated with the later cars. This model was sometimes known as the Coachbuilt Saloon to distinguish it from the Fabric-bodied type.

TYPE RG FABRIC SALOON, 1930-1931 (MAY 1930)

The Fabric Saloon that replaced the RF type in May 1930 was known as the RG type, and was contemporary with the steel-panelled RL Saloon. It was not in production for long before being replaced by the Type RH. A total of just 1200 examples is estimated to have been built before production was brought to a halt in January 1931.

Unlike the RL Saloon that it broadly resembled, the RG was built on an ash frame, suitably reinforced in some areas to compensate for the loss of the metal panels' stiffening effect. An attractive distinguishing feature between the two was that the fabric-bodied car had two lines of piping running around the body at waist level while the RL had a conventional single moulding.

Development during production included the arrival of bonnet louvres at the same time as on the RL, and a change to a longer scuttle just as production was ending in January 1931. Early cars had no scuttle ventilators, but the later ones did have them.

As on the RL, a smoker's vent could be fitted to the roof, unless the car had been ordered with a sliding sunroof panel. Bryan Purves estimated that around 10% of RG models had the sliding roof, which added £5 to the cost of the car. That was initially £140, but was reduced to £130 at the start of September 1930.

The waist rail in contrasting colour was a nice touch on the RG Fabric Saloon.

TYPE VD DELIVERY VAN, 1930-1931 (JUNE 1930)

By spring 1930, Austin had decided to take production of the Austin Seven Delivery Van in-house, and the model they called the Type VD replaced the Startin-built vans that had been offered up to that point. In general, it was based on the new Type RL Saloon that had been introduced in May 1930, and was introduced a month after it.

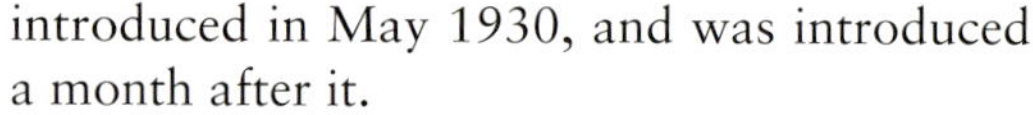

The Type VD van was quite square-cut in comparison with earlier designs and, like the Gordon England and Startin's new own-design vans, had an enclosed cab. The long cab doors were those of the RL Saloon with winding windows and a cut-out around the rear mudguard, and the tail doors had oval windows. There was also a scuttle ventilator on the driver's side. These vans had steel panels on an ash frame and were in production until January 1931. Only about 100 were built before a larger-capacity van on the new longer wheelbase replaced this model.

The first Austin Seven Delivery Van built in-house at Longbridge was the Type VD – often called the RL type after the Saloon on which it was based. These steel-bodied vans had a decidedly more functional look that the pretty design that had been built by Startin.

TYPE AF TOURER, 1930 (JUNE 1930)

The AF was the first tourer with the tall radiator, short scuttle and long bonnet, and retained the alloy bodywork of the AE. Its general appearance was very much like that of its predecessor, the AE, although the bonnet sides were louvred like those on the contemporary RM saloons.

The AF models began at around chassis number 111000, and had a five-gallon petrol tank, a petrol tap with a "reserve" position, and a dial-type oil gauge on the dash. The very first ones probably did not have the coupled braking system, but the majority did. Austin dropped the showroom price even lower, to £118, which was a very sensible move in view of the effect that the Wall Street crash of November 1929 was beginning to have on car sales generally.

The AF was very different from the preceding AE, notably the tall radiator and short scuttle, but retained alloy body-panels. (Clive Barker)

TYPE PB TWO-SEATER, 1930-1931 (JUNE 1930)

Priced at the same £130 as its predecessor and still with a boat-tailed body, the PB Two-seater took over from the PA in June 1930 and was in production until January 1931 (although some experts suggest it lasted until the middle of that year).

The major difference between the PA and the PB was that the PB had a shorter scuttle. The very earliest cars had plain bonnet sides, with louvred bonnet sides arriving in September 1930, when the showroom price was reduced to £122 10s 0d.

The Two-seater evolved into a Type PB in June 1930, and this early example, with plain bonnet sides, is seen with its hood erected.

TYPE VA/VB/VC MILK DELIVERY CARS, 1930-1931

Austin's decision to build the Delivery Van versions of the Seven themselves may have prompted the development of a second light commercial derivative that was called the Milk Delivery Car (MDC). This was based on the contemporary Tourer rather than on the Saloon.

The first 24 examples were known as VA types and were built in July and August 1930 on what must have been left-over chassis for the AE Tourer (which had given way to the AF from June 1930). A second version, the VB, entered production in September and was based on the AF Tourer. It lasted until December 1930, when a third version of the MDC was introduced. There were probably at least 115 VB versions of the model.

The Milk Delivery Car was one of the more intriguing versions of the Seven. It was based on the contemporary Tourer.

The MDC was initially priced at £125 and was essentially a Seven Tourer with the rear of the hood arranged to fold up and a hinged "tailgate" that gave access to milk crates or churns stowed in the body behind the seats. The rear wheelarches, passenger compartment floors and rear floors were all reinforced, and the passenger seat was removable to create more load space within the body. It's possible that some Type-VCs had steel body panels, but all Type-VB were in alloy. All models were fitted with lower than standard rear axle gearing.

The change from Type AF to Type AG Tourer in January 1931 of course had a knock-on effect on the Milk Delivery Car. So from that month, the light commercial derivative was redesignated a Type VC.

Its configuration was essentially unchanged, although like its parent AG Tourer it had the same longer scuttle as the RM Saloon. At some point during 1931, the price of the MDC was reduced to £112 10s 0d. Production is thought to have ended in August 1931 after about 1100 had been made, and the VC model was not directly replaced. Perhaps sales were slow; certainly, at least one example is known not to have been registered until 1932.

The Milk Delivery Car was essentially a Seven Tourer with the rear of the hood arranged to fold up and a hinged "tailgate" that gave access to milk crates or churns stowed in the body behind the seats. This is a VB with its tall radiator. (Matthew Barker)

"Milk Delivery The Austin Way Saves Time, Money and Labour". The Milk Delivery Car remained available through 1931, and the last examples were not registered until the following year.

TYPE RM SALOON, 1931-1932 (JANUARY 1931)

January 1931 brought several new models of Seven, central to which was a successor to the Type RL Saloon that was logically named the RM type. This and its accompanying fabric-panelled Type RH were the last Seven Saloons built on the original 75-inch wheelbase. Their production began just before the last of the RL Saloons were built.

The RM once again had a steel-panelled body, was similar to the RL but now with 8-inch scuttle and 25½-inch bonnet (all RLs had a 6-inch scuttle and 27½-inch bonnet). As first put on sale, it cost the same £130, and the same £5 extra was asked for a sliding roof. From the start of September 1931 its base price was reduced to £118, and a month later it was fitted with the latest Lucas-Graves twin-filament headlamps and the redesigned front wings that characterised the RN replacement models introduced the same month. The last RM Saloons were probably built in February 1932.

First registered in April 1931, this well-presented car is an example of the steel-panelled RM Saloon. (Robert Knight)

TYPE RH FABRIC SALOON, 1931 (JANUARY 1931)

The steel-panelled RM Saloon was of course matched by a fabric-bodied equivalent, and this took the type name of RH. It was a short-lived model that was only in production from January to July 1931, and it would be the last fabric-bodied Seven Saloon from Longbridge. Bryan Purves quotes a production total of just 484 examples, although Graham Baldock (*Identifying Austin Sevens from their Factory Initials*) puts the total at around 700.

Most of the features of the RG Saloon were similar to those of the contemporary steel-panelled RM, but unfortunately there are no known survivors of the model to provide a more detailed understanding of it.

TYPE VE DELIVERY VAN, 1931 (JANUARY 1931)

When the RM Saloon replaced the RL type in January 1931, the Delivery Van based on the Saloon chassis of course changed to the new specification.

The new van was known as a VE type and remained in production until November 1931. Very much the same as the VD that it replaced, it now had the longer scuttle of the RM Saloon and also had rectangular windows rather than oval ones in the tail doors.

TYPE AG TOURER, 1931-1932 (JANUARY 1931)

A 1931 Type AG Tourer. The AG represented the last of the small-door Tourers on the 75-inch wheelbase. (RS Vintage)

The AG Tourer was introduced in January 1931 and went out of production in June 1932. These steel-bodied cars were the last of the small-door Tourers, and the last Tourers on the 75in wheelbase.

Their specification generally corresponded with that of the contemporary RM saloons, and they shared the same longer scuttle, shorter louvred bonnet and the same radiator surround. They had similar rectangular doors, too. The scuttle-mounted petrol tank had a tap that gave access to a reserve. The body was distinguished by two vertical seams on the tail panel. The showroom price was now down at £110.

From this angle you can just about make out the two vertical seams on the tail panel that distinguish this model. (RS Vintage)

TYPE PC TWO-SEATER, 1931-1932 (JANUARY 1931)

The Type PC was the last of the Two-seaters with the boat-tailed body and was introduced in January 1931 (or, according to some experts, mid-1931). The body had a short scuttle and bonnet louvres like that of the later Type PBs. The front wing design changed in November 1931.

The first of these cars cost the same as the outgoing PB but their price was reduced to £118 in September 1931. They then remained in production until September 1932, retaining their original 75in wheelbase at a time when other models were changing to the later longer wheelbase. Production figures of 559 for 1931 and 476 for 1932 have been suggested.

The basic shape of the Two-Seater remained unchanged for the Type PC announced in January 1931.

This 1932 brochure shows an interior as well as a side profile artwork. The price had been dropped from £122 10s 0d to £118 in September 1931.

The SEVEN TWO-SEATER

WITH AMPLE LEG ROOM AND ADJUSTABLE DRIVING SEAT

PIONEERS

A two-seater model of this light, swift, easily managed car, was certain of a popular reception. "Sporty" in appearance, with bright and cheerful colouring it made instant appeal to those who do not require a car to seat more than two. The car is not only fast, it is extremely comfortable to travel in, and even after a long day's run there is no undue fatigue. The well upholstered seats are of ample proportions; and access or exit is very easy, for the doors are wide.

When the weather is inclement the easily erected hood and side curtains give full protection.

Behind the seats a suit or week-end case may be carried, and in addition, there is room for a considerable amount of luggage in the compartment at the rear of the car. The spare wheel is also carried here, and is easily taken out when required.

The two-seater is a smart car which is a strong favourite with the young folk.

Completely equipped, including electric starting and lighting, dipping beam device for headlamps, air strangler, electric horn, speedometer, driving mirror, windscreen wiper, licence holder, shock absorbers, spare wheel and tyre, and blank number plates

THE AUSTIN SEVEN

Page Eight

STEPHENSON

PIONEERS

Opened first railway —Stockton to Darlington, 1825.

PRICE AT WORKS

£118.0.0

ALL EXTERIOR FITTINGS CHROMIUM PLATED

TRIPLEX GLASS THROUGHOUT

THE FIRST—AND STILL THE FIRST

Page Nine

TYPE PF & PL TWO-SEATERS, 1931 (JANUARY 1931)

Although there is no physical evidence (no survivors, no photos) that there were any further factory variants of the boat-tail two seater, there are two other type codes mentioned in the Longbridge records, both with a fabric finish. Factory notes indicate that the PF had fabric covering over metal panels, and the PL would have had all-fabric panels, which must have made it a rather lighter contstruction. These models were doubtless intended to cater for buyers who preferred the fabric-panelled styles of the 1920s to the newer metal-panelled styles. This was no means the first time Austin had made fabric-bodied and metal-panelled versions of the same design available; as explained above, from May 1930 there were fabric (RG) and steel (RL) versions of the same Saloon design on offer. If they ever made it into production, the PF and PL models presumably would have finished at the same time as the PC in 1932.

EXPERIMENTAL SIX-WHEEL TIPPER LORRY, 1931

Austin continued to investigate options for commercial derivatives of the Seven, and in 1931 examined the possibility of a six-wheel chassis. The idea was not entirely new, and as long ago as 1927 a designer called Gardiner, from Andover, had developed a prototype three-axle commercial chassis from a 1926 Type AD Tourer. There is some evidence of limited production.

The 1931 Austin prototype was based on a Type VD Delivery Van, with its back body removed and steel chassis extensions added. A third, undriven axle was added (giving a total wheelbase of 115 inches) and was fitted with cable-operated brakes. A wooden dropside tipper body was then added behind the driving "cab". No production followed, and the prototype seems to have ended its days as a runabout at the Longbridge factory.

Probably built in 1931, the six-wheel lorry was another Austin investigation into commercial-vehicle possibilities.

Production totals, 1926-1931

Below are the generally accepted annual production figures for the Austin Seven. Individual type totals are available for 1928-1931 and are shown in a separate table below.

1926	13,174
1927	21,671
1928	24,247
1929	26,540
1930	23,739
1931	20,645

Some individual type totals were compiled by RJ Wyatt for his 1982 book, *Austin Seven – The Motor for the Million*. Wyatt was well aware that his figures were incomplete and in some cases were approximations, but they have generally been accepted as presenting a reasonably accurate guide.

	1928	1929	1930	1931
Chassis	2719	4430	1528	752
Tourers	8233	5304	3187	1647
Saloons	2142	3607	11,101	12,758
De Luxe Saloons				2970
Fabric Saloons	4331	8309	5120	782
Two-seaters		107	425	559
Coupés	51	347	127	7
Delivery Vans (Austin)		1	115	1144
Delivery Vans (Startin)	316	391	631	50
Sports		1	48	97
Super Sports		2		

These individual totals help to illustrate the rise to dominance of the Saloon models in this period and the slow decline in popularity of the Tourers.

Identification, 1926-1931

Austin Sevens in this period are usually identified by their Car Number, which is shown on the service plate. Up to May 1927, this was a zinc disc that was screwed to the left-hand door pillar, and after that date it was an oblong plate that was riveted to the scuttle.

Car Numbers consist of a sequence prefix (eg A9) followed by a four-digit serial number between 101 and 9999. Car Numbers and Chassis Numbers matched up to the end of the A2 series, but this was no longer the case from the start of the A3 series in early summer 1926. Engine Numbers had a separate and unrelated sequence.

The sequence prefixes relevant to the 1926-1931 period are:

A2	commencing May 1925
A3	May 1926
A4	February 1927
A5	August 1927
A6	April 1928
A7	September 1928
A8	February 1929
A9	June 1929
B	October 1929
B1	March 1930
B2	September 1930
B3	January 1931
B4	May 1931

Build records for some cars from this period still survive and are held by the British Motor Industry Heritage Trust at the British Motor Museum in Gaydon.

The surviving records are for the following:

Car Numbers	Chassis numbers	Dates
A8-101 to A8-9999	77535 to 87433	31 Jan 1929 to June 1929
A9-101 to A9-9999	87434 to 97332	June to October 1929
B1-101 to B1-9999	107228 to 117126	March to September 1930
B3-101 to B3-9999	1270126 to 136924	January to May 1931

Technical Specifications, 1926-1931

Engine: Four-cylinder side-valve, two main bearings

Capacity: 747.5ccc

Bore x stroke: 56mm x 76mm

Induction: 1926-1928: Zenith type 22FZ carburettor (bronze body); 1929 and export from 1930: Zenith type 22FZB carburettor (Mazak body); some cars from November 1930: Amal carburettor

Power: 13bhp at 2400rpm; Type EA Ulster 24bhp at 5000rpm (unsupercharged), 27bhp at 4500rm (supercharged)

Gearbox: Three-speed with reverse. 3.20:1, 1.80:1, 1.00:1; reverse 4.28:1

Axle ratio: Standard 4.9:1, Sports 4.4:1 (to 1928) 5.67:1 (from 1928), Milk Delivery Car 5.625:1

Brakes: Drums all round, initially 6in x 1in; 7in x 1in standard from September 1926' Footbrake operated rear pair and handbrake operated front pair before July 1930, when coupled brakes became standard (both handbrake and footbrake then acted on all four wheels).

Steering: Worm and wheel type

Front suspension: Beam axle with transverse leaf spring and radius arms

Rear suspension: Beam axle with quarter-elliptic leaf springs

Wheels and tyres: Wire spoked wheels with 26in diameter to March 1926 and 19in dia. thereafter. From early 1924 – 26in x 3½in tyres; From March 1926 – 19 x 3.50 tyres

Length: 106in/2692mm (typical)

Wheelbase: 75in/1905mm

Width: 46in/1168mm (typical)

Front Track: 40in/1016mm

Rear Track: 43in/1092mm

Weight: 800lb approx

THE LONG-WHEELBASE MODELS

October 1931 marked the beginning of another major stage in the story of the Austin Seven, as the first models with the new and longer 81-inch wheelbase entered production. The increase in size no doubt reflected customer demand for more passenger space, but it also had the benefit of making the Seven a more appealing proposition at a time when the British car industry was suffering from the effects of the Depression that had been triggered by the 1929 Wall Street Crash.

Even so, the autumn of 1931 brought the start of gradual change rather than an abrupt transition. The new cars did not look very different from their forebears, and of course several of the older models on the 75-inch wheelbase remained available alongside the first of the new 81-inch wheelbase types; their time would not be over until the autumn of 1932. There were six of these "overlap" models: the VC Milk Delivery Car remained available until August 1931; the VE Delivery Van until mid-1932 (possibly as late as September); the EA "Ulster" Sports until January 1932; the RM Saloon until February 1932; and the AG Tourer and the PC Two-seater until September 1932.

Very clear from the sales figures quoted later in this Chapter is that there was a noticeable increase in demand for the Two-seater models. However, it is important to see this in its proper context: the British Army put in large orders for specially adapted Two-seaters from 1933, and these of course inflated the production and sales numbers. The military models are not discussed in this Chapter, but are treated separately along with other military types in Chapter 6.

The period of the original long-wheelbase models was a brief one in the timeline of the

Ideals of the mid-Thirties: a Nippy and a tennis match in the beautiful English countryside.

Austin Seven. It began to draw to a close in summer 1934 when the first of the further redesigned models came on-stream, but of course production of some of the older models continued so that there was an overlap with the new-look Sevens.

Minor changes were made on production as they were needed, but there were also some more major ones. Perhaps the most impact was made by the changes in September 1932, which were headlined by a new four-speed gearbox in place of the three-speed type and a rear-mounted five-gallon petrol tank in pace of the scuttle-mounted tank. At the same time, a new Zenith 26VA side-draught carburettor became standard.

The first four-speed gearboxes had no synchromesh, but from September 1933 synchromesh was fitted on third and fourth gears; as usual, the Delivery Vans lagged a little behind other models because they were using up old-stock parts, and the first four-speed Delivery Van was not built until December. At an undetermined point during 1934, Austin then made left-hand-drive chassis available for export. Some were used for the Sports models, but there was also a batch of left-hand-drive Delivery Vans in April that year.

Another reminder of tranquil times in the Thirties: an AVH Delivery Van goes about its business.

TYPE RN SALOON, 1931-1932 (OCTOBER 1931)

The RN Saloon introduced in October 1931 was the first one to use the new longer-wheelbase (81in) chassis, and its body had been redesigned to make good use of the extra six inches available. It was not only longer, but wider, too. The design of the rear seat had been greatly improved and legroom was further increased with the addition of footwells. The extra body length also allowed the doors to finish ahead of the rear wheel arch, with vertical rather than shaped rear faces, and this in turn allowed winding windows to be fitted.

These bodies were readily recognisable by the two vertical seams on the rear panel. In the beginning, all of them had an Austin-made sliding roof, but in approximately April 1932 a solid-roof version became available with the name of Standard Saloon. This was probably introduced to fill a gap in the range left by the recent demise of the RL with its solid-roof option. By September 1932, the two vertical seams at the rear had disappeared as the body began to presage the changes that would be made for its successor.

Production of the RN Saloon ended in October 1932, and that month the model was superseded by the RP type. However, supplies of parts for the new RP model had started to arrive at Longbridge by about August, and Austin took the decision to update the last of the RNs by building them with the new four-speed gearbox and rear-mounted fuel tank. As a result, the final RN Saloons had an interesting hybrid specification.

The RN Saloon was the first one with the longer 81in wheelbase. (Clive Barker)

TYPE VG DELIVERY VAN, 1932-1933 (MID-1932)

The Austin Seven Delivery Van on offer between mid-1932 and January 1933 was a VG model, and was based on the new RN Saloon that had entered production in October 1931. Like the new Saloon, the new Delivery Van had the longer 81in wheelbase, which of course provided more carrying capacity for the van body. Load space was now claimed to be 46 cu ft, and the latest van could haul a weight of more than 5 cwt (560 lb, 254kg).

The VG was the first long-wheelbase van and was related to the contemporary RN Saloon. This is a late example, registered in January 1934, and has been made available as a scale model.

Despite being based on the RN, the VG used the older RM-pattern wings and had scuttle ventilators on both sides. These vans had a higher roof than the ones they replaced, and the longer wheelbase allowed the cab doors to finish ahead of the rear wings. There were rectangular windows in the tail doors, and the spare wheel was now carried against the side of the body behind the passenger's seat. Like their parent Saloons, these vans had a vacuum-operated windscreen wiper and a hinged scuttle ventilator on the driver's side.

The VG and AVG vans were supplied in grey primer for £110 or in one of four factory-mandated colours for £113. Austin would of course paint the vehicles to suit the customer's wishes, but special paint finishes cost an extra £5, and no doubt that charge was levied on each one that the Automobile Association bought for its road service division. The best estimate is that around 2300 examples of the VG vans were built before production ended in early 1933.

THE TYPE RP SALOON, 1932-1934 (OCTOBER 1932)

The key changes developed for the Type RP Saloon were mechanical rather than visual. On the one hand, a four-speed constant-mesh gearbox replaced the old three-speed type; and on the other longer rear side rails supported a new rear-mounted 5-gallon petrol tank and a positive-acting AC fuel pump was mounted on the engine. There were new and wider brake drums, too, with a 1¼in width instead of the earlier 1in width. The RP was introduced in October 1932 and remained in production for just under two years, the last ones being built in August 1934.

This was to be the last of the "box" Saloons, as the model that replaced it would have much more modern styling. Its body was very similar to that of the RN Saloon that it replaced, but

The RP was the last of the "Box" Saloon Sevens. This example was registered in 1934. (RS Vintage)

the rear end had been revised. It lost the visible body seams together with an inch in width, and the rear panel was rather more upright.

The usual round of modifications followed as production went on. The gearbox gained synchromesh on third and fourth gears in August 1933. From October 1933, the De Luxe models gained a cover over the rear-mounted spare wheel, and all RPs were given revised door trim panels. In December, scuttle-mounted semaphore trafficators became standard, and then from July 1934 the gearbox was further revised with the addition of synchromesh on second gear.

There were always two models available, known as the Standard and De Luxe types; the De Luxe was the more popular, and during 1932 accounted for about 80% of total sales. Standard models initially cost £115, a figure that was increased to £118 in August 1933. The De Luxe models had real hide upholstery instead of leathercloth, plus a Pytchley sunshine roof and Triplex safety glass. These cost £125 when first available, and £128 from August 1933.

TYPE AH TOURER, 1932-1934 (SEPTEMBER 1932)

The Type AH was the open derivative of the contemporary RP saloon. (Robin Lawton)

The Tourers gained the new 81in wheelbase chassis in September 1932, a year after it had first appeared for Saloons. The new long-wheelbase model was designated the Type AH. (Note that some commentators suggest a June 1932 start to production.) This was the open derivative of the contemporary RP saloon and now had its 5-gallon petrol tank mounted at the rear of the chassis, with the filler on the right-hand side.

The external body seams of the Type AG were now concealed, and the doors were once again more or less square; exterior door handles were set vertically again. The scuttle was like that of the RN saloon but was not extended upwards to carry the windscreen, and the bonnet and radiator surround were also like those of the RN. From December 1932, a distinctive black band was painted on the waist moulding, and production lasted until July 1934.

The first of these Tourers with the rear-mounted petrol tank was on chassis number 159534. For many years, they were mistakenly described as AJ types, but in fact no such type existed.

TYPE PD TWO-SEATER, 1932-1934 (SEPTEMBER 1932)

The next generation of the Two-seater Seven was designed around the new long-wheelbase chassis with rear-mounted petrol tank, and was known as the PD type. The body was quite different from the ones that had gone before, with a neat tail that curved downwards and no trace of the earlier boat-tail design. The spare wheel was mounted on the outside of this new tail, and the only access to the luggage space now provided was from inside the passenger compartment. The longer wheelbase allowed for rectangular doors with no need for cut-outs around the rear wheel arches. These models had detachable side-screens that folded in half vertically so that either the rear seat or the front compartment could have open sides while the other section remained closed.

Production ran until summer 1934, and there was also a military variant of the PD which is covered in Chapter 6. The civilian version was priced at £105, but the British Army managed to get their bulk order at a preferential rate of £85 14s 9d each!

Straight edges at the rear of the doors were just one feature that distinguished the PD Two-seater from its predecessors. The new tail was neat and practical, too.

TYPE EB "65" SPORTS TOURER, 1933-1934 (JUNE 1933)

The Type EB was not at all the same kind of car as the EA Ulster, but was an attractive sporty model with a top speed of 65mph, from which it took its other name of the 65 Sports Tourer.

The Sports model that followed the Ulster was a very much tamer machine, which traded perhaps on the image that the Ulster had created but was intended as a sporty looking car for everyday use. Introduced in June 1933, it was initially known as the 65 Sports Tourer, and it took the logical next name on from the Type EA Ulster, becoming the Type EB.

The number 65 was used to indicate the car's 65mph top speed, in much the same way as for the earlier 50mph Sports model.

The "65" had some engine modifications that boosted power to 23bhp at 4800rpm, including a Zenith downdraught carburettor, a raised compression ratio, special valves, and a high-lift camshaft. The lubrication system was improved, too, with a one-gallon ribbed sump and machined con-rods with oil feeds to the gudgeon pins. This model had a Burgess silencer and the drop-centre front axle from the Ulster, which gave it a suitably sporting sound and demeanour. A close-ratio gearbox added to the sporting feel, and the first cars had 5.66:1 axle gearing. The synchromesh gearbox was fitted from August 1933, and later models changed to the standard 5.25:1 rear axle gearing.

The body was built from aluminium panels on a steel floorpan, with a rounded tail, full-depth doors which had sloping tops rather than elbow cutaways, and steel cycle-style wings painted in the usual black to contrast with the body. Luggage was stowed in a compartment

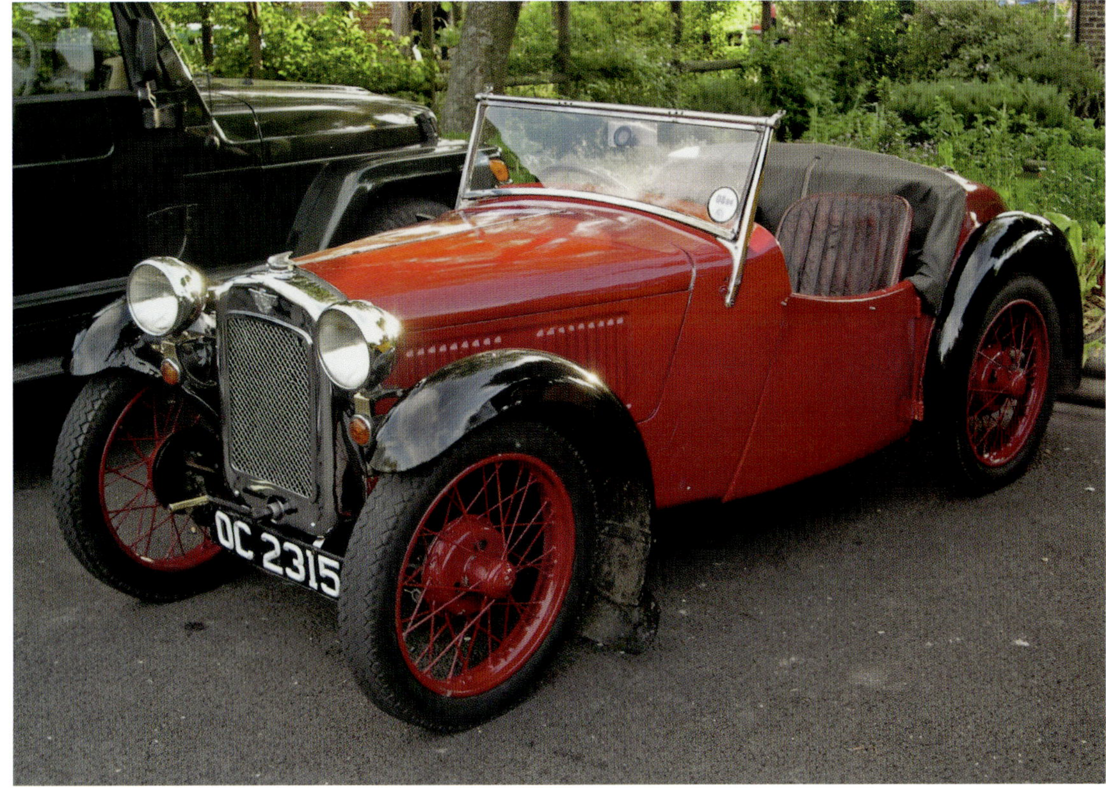

The body was of the Type EB built from aluminium panels on a steel floorpan, with a rounded tail, full-depth doors which had sloping tops rather than elbow cutaways, and steel cycle-style wings painted in the usual black to contrast with the body. (Clive Barker)

in the tail that could only be reached from inside the car and was separated from the boot, whose drop-down lid gave access only to the spare wheel and tools.

These cars cost £152, and were available with LHD for countries such as Germany. Approximately 275 were made in all before production ended in January 1934.

TYPE AVH DELIVERY VAN, 1933-1935 (JANUARY 1933)

The RP Saloon replaced the RN type on production in October 1932, but this time there was a slight delay before the vans took on the new specification. The AVH model did not enter production until January 1933, and remained available for two years until it was replaced in January 1935. Its cargo capacity was now claimed to be 51½ cu ft.

There were several important changes from the earlier Type AVG Delivery Van. First of all, the AVH had the RP Saloon's new four-speed gearbox instead of the old three-speed type. It had a high frame, with the spare wheel, jack and tool kit all carried below the floor at the rear. There were ventilating louvres above the

The 1933 Type AVH Delivery Van was based on the RP Saloon and of course had the latest 81in wheelbase. (Clive Barker)

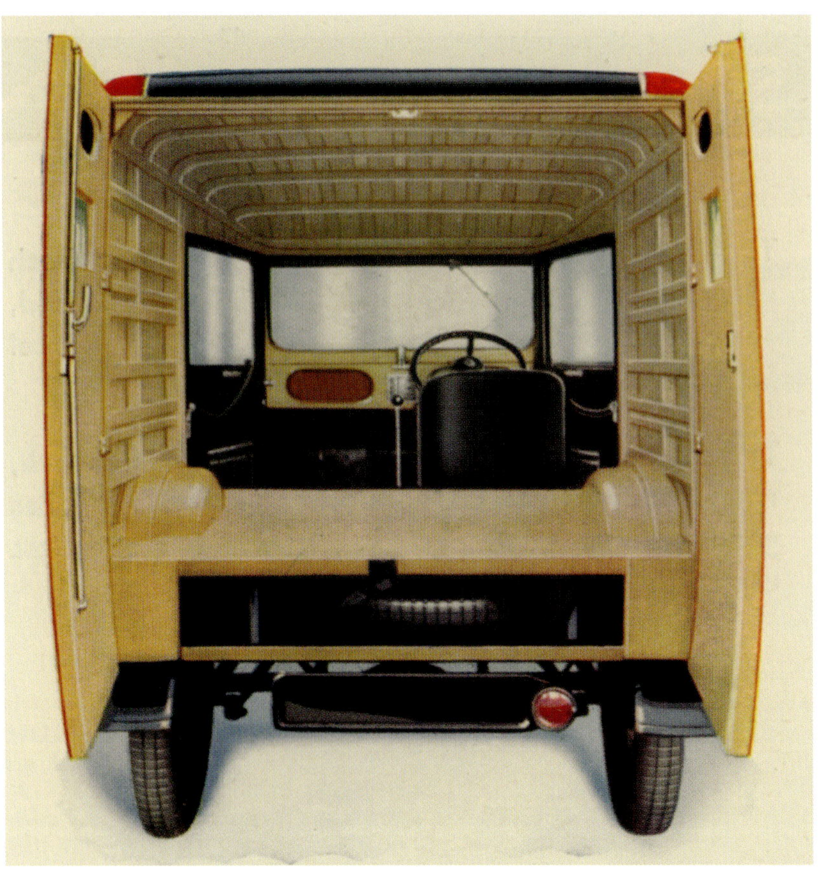

tail door windows, and the roof was covered in leathercloth. The driver benefited from a fully adjustable seat, but the separate passenger's seat was now an extra-cost option. Early models used left-over RN-style instruments in a special panel, as well as an RN-type chrome-plated radiator shell and an AH-type louvred bonnet. The wings were of the RN/RP type. Later models, with the RP-type instumentation, including a fuel gauge, also featured a special fuel tank with its sender unit and outlet pipe outside the cab.

Production changes followed those on the parent Saloons, and the original constant-mesh gearbox gave way in February 1934 to one with synchromesh on third and fourth gears. From April 1934, LHD vans were available for export. Prices on the Home Market remained as before, at £113 in one of the four "factory" colours or £110 in primer finish, but later models were priced at £108.

Austin claimed even more cargo space than before in the back of the AVH Delivery Van.

THE TYPE AEB NIPPY, 1934-1937 (JANUARY 1934)

As its AEB designation suggests, the Nippy was closely related to the earlier EB or 65 model. Three-letter codes were new for 1934, and the AEB was introduced in January that year. The price was initially £142, but by October 1936 this had dropped to £130.

Where the Nippy differed from the 65 that it closely resembled was in having steel body

The 1934 Nippy had a similar appearance to the earlier EB, but was recognisable by the sidelights on the wing crowns.

panels, and in having sidelights mounted on the wing crowns. This model was really aimed at customers who wanted the looks but were less interested in the actual performance; for those who wanted performance as well, there was the contemporary AEK Speedy.

Like its EB predecessor, the AEB Nippy was built with LHD for export, notably to Germany; one was displayed at the Berlin Motor Show in 1935. From February 1936, Nippy engines gained the forced-feed lubrication system that was already in use on the higher-performance Speedy engines, and by October 1936 it was possible to order a Nippy with the Speedy engine for an extra £12 10s 0d.

About 800 Nippy models were made before production ended in June 1937. According to *Motor Sport* for December 1938, 19 unused Nippy bodies were sold to the well-known body "broker" Cooper's of Putney for £20 each, and these doubtless found their way onto a variety of chassis for which they had not originally been intended.

Front and rear three-quarter view of a 1936 AEB Nippy. (Robin Lawton)

TYPE EK SPORTS 75, 1934 (APRIL 1934)

The mantle of the EB Sports 65 passed in April 1934 to the Type EK or Sports 75, of which the prototype had been built in January. This was another aluminium-panelled two-seater, this time with shorter doors and deep sill panels below them, plus a pointed rather than rounded tail. A vee screen added to the sporty appearance, but the impressive-looking racing filler cap was really for show, and a standard-capacity five-gallon tank was fitted. There was also an element of comfort and practicality in the large wind deflector valances that were mounted outboard of the

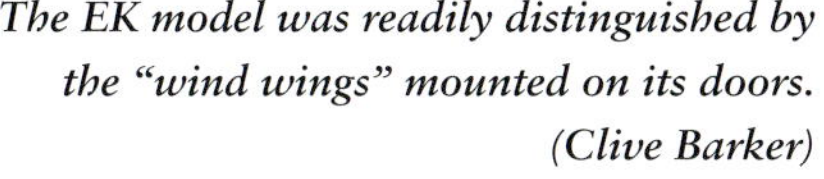

The EK model was readily distinguished by the "wind wings" mounted on its doors. (Clive Barker)

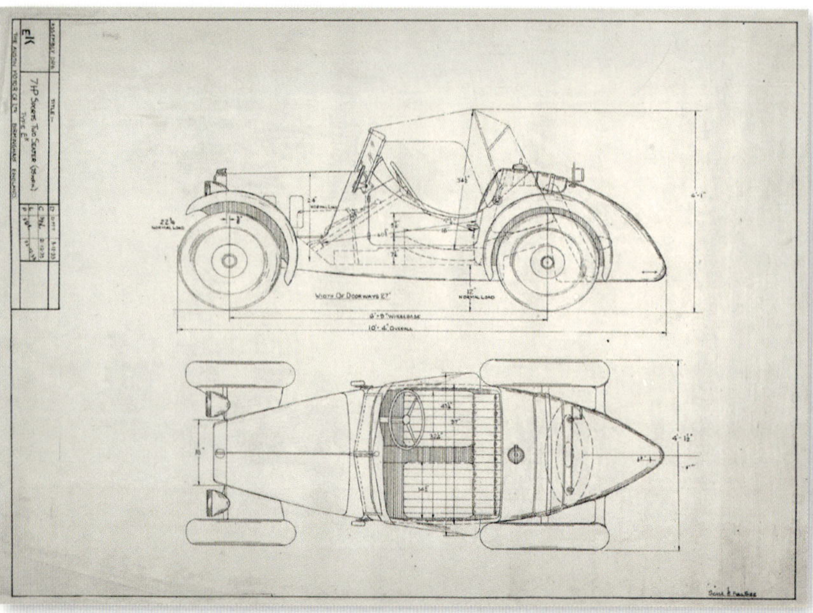

Austin's drawings for the EK show a side profile and an overhead view.

elbow cutouts on the door tops.

In theory, the car could reach 75mph (hence the name). To the modifications seen on the EB's engine it added pressure-lubricated big ends, but with just 23bhp the EK was never intended for competition work. Only 40 examples were made before June 1934, when the model was renamed the AEK Speedy under the new three-letter system.

The valances on the door cutouts are clear in this photo. (Matthew Barker)

Identification, 1931-1934

Austin Sevens are usually identified by their Car Number, which is shown on the service plate. This is an oblong plate that is riveted to the scuttle.

Car Numbers consist of a sequence prefix (eg B5) followed by a four-digit serial number between 101 and 9999. Note that Car Numbers and Chassis Numbers did not match in this period, and that Engine Numbers also had their own separate sequence.

The sequence prefixes relevant to the 1931-1934 period are:

B4	commencing May 1931
B5	January 1932
B6	June 1932
B7	January 1933
B8	June 1933
B9	January 1934
C	June 1934

No build records survive for cars from this period.

Production totals, 1931-1934

Below are the generally accepted annual production figures for the Austin Seven. Individual type totals are available for 1931-1934 and are shown in a separate table below.

1931	20,645
1932	21,285
1933	20,383
1934	22,685

Some individual type totals were compiled by RJ Wyatt for his 1982 book, *Austin Seven – The Motor for the Million*. Wyatt was well aware that his figures were incomplete and in some cases were approximations, but they have generally been accepted as presenting a reasonably accurate guide. The figures for the 1931 calendar year are shown in Chapter 4.

	1932	1933	1934
Chassis	620	789	713
Tourers	1062	1484	1449
Saloons	2998	2765	2901
De Luxe Saloons	12,434	11,837	13,638
Two-seaters	476	865	1015
Delivery Vans (Austin)	2364	2497	2380
Sports	22	234	228

These individual totals once again show how Saloon models had come to dominate production. Also striking is the marked preference for the better-equipped De Luxe models.

Note that there were also some Cabriolet models in 1934, but these were introduced in the latter part of the calendar-year and are therefore discussed in the next Chapter.

Technical Specifications, 1931-1934

Engine: Four-cylinder side-valve, two main bearings

Capacity: 747.5ccc

Bore x stroke: 56mm x 76mm

Induction: to 1932: Zenith type 22FZB carburettor (Mazak body); from September 1932: Zenith type 26VA carburettor; some cars: Amal carburettor

Power: 13bhp at 2400rpm;
21bhp at 4400rpm (Nippy),
23bhp at 4800rpm (Type EB)

Gearbox: to 1932 – three-speed with reverse. Gear ratios – 3.20:1, 1.80:1, 1.00:1; reverse 4.28:1
from 1932 – four-speed with reverse, Gear ratios – 4.37:1, 2.64:1, 1.66:1, 1.00:1; reverse 5.62:1
Close-ratio gearbox ratios 4.04:1, 2.35:1, 1.48:1, 1.00:1; reverse 4.98:1
No synchromesh 1932-33, Synchromesh on 3rd and 4th 1933-34

Axle ratio: Standard 4.9:1 (to 1932), 5.25:1 (from 1932); Sports 5.67:1 (to 1932) 5.625:1 (from 1932) except 5.66:1 on Type 65 EB models, Milk Delivery Car 5.625:1

Brakes: Drums all round, 7in x 1in to September 1932; 7in x 1¼in from September 1932. Coupled brakes (both handbrake and footbrake act on all four wheels)

Steering: Worm and wheel type

Front suspension: Beam axle with transverse leaf spring and radius arms

Rear suspension: Beam axle with quarter-elliptic leaf springs

Wheels and tyres: Rubery Owen Magna wire wheels with Staybrite centres from June 1931, 19in x 3.50 tyres

Length: 112in/2845mm (typical)
121in/3073mm (AVH Delivery Van)

Wheelbase: 81in/2057mm

Width: 46in/1168mm (typical)
53in/1346mm (AVH Van)

Front Track: 40in/1016mm

Rear Track: 43in/1092mm

Weight: 800lb approx (typical)

THE FINAL FIVE YEARS, 1934-1939

As usual, the changeover to the new models was gradual rather than abrupt, and several of the older Seven types remained available alongside them for some time. The "overlap" models this time were the Type AVH Delivery Van, which did not go out of production until January 1935, the Type AEK or Speedy (which had earlier been the Type EK), and the Type AEB or Nippy Sports, which lasted all the way through to June 1937. Three-letter type codes gradually became the norm for all new models.

The most obvious change from July 1934 was the introduction of a new front end design, where the radiator was concealed behind a styled, sloping cowl that was painted to match the bodywork. This was not universal at first, but was gradually rolled out across the range. July 1934 also brought some important chassis changes that allowed the cars to sit much lower than their predecessors. The so-called "low frame" cars had smaller (17in) road wheels and revised springs that reduced the overall height – although in practice some of the first low frame models used old-style 19in wheels. The last of the older "high frame" models was built in 1936 – except, of course, for the Delivery Vans, which continued to be assembled using old-stock components and did not switch to the low frame until 1937.

There were other changes in the summer of 1934. Within a few weeks of the new Ruby Saloons being introduced, the gearbox was modified to incorporate synchromesh on second

A Pearl Cabriolet on a lovely summer's day. (Matthew Barker)

gear as well as third and fourth – except once again on the Delivery Vans, which retained the older gearbox for more than a year as supplies were gradually used up.

Brake leverage was improved in June and July 1935 (but in September for Delivery Vans), and Export models were given stronger front springs at the same time. During 1936, a foot-operated dipswitch introduced with the Ruby improved the driver's convenience, and in June came an important change to the engine when a third crankshaft bearing was added to improve durability and smoothness. The electrical system was improved at the same time by the introduction of a dynamo.

From October 1935, hourglass steering was progressively introduced. Then in December 1937, the standard axle gearing was changed to 5.125:1, a ratio which it retained until production of all Sevens ended in 1939.

This 1934 chassis displays the new cowled radiator grille that came to characterise the later Sevens.

TYPE ARQ RUBY SALOON, 1934-1936 (JULY 1934)

The Saloon range was completely transformed in July 1934 with the introduction of the ARQ model, which was also given one of the "jewel" names favoured that year and became the Ruby. As before, there were both Standard and De Luxe variants, and the latter proved by far the more popular. A small quantity of Standard models was built for export with left-hand-drive.

These cars looked lower and sleeker than their predecessors, and one reason was that the chassis rode much closer to the ground. Thanks to revised road springs and smaller-diameter wheels, the floor level was all of five inches lower than before, and the tool box and battery were moved from below the seats to new locations on the bulkhead to allow this. In practice, the first cars were delivered with old-style 19in wheels, but production soon standardised on a 17in size. 18in wheels were exclusively used on home-market vans and export Rubies were normally fitted with 16in wheels.. The gearbox was the latest four-speed type with synchromesh on 2nd, 3rd and top gears.

The Saloon body was once again constructed with steel panels over an ash frame, but it was more curvaceous than before and featured a fashionable semi-swept tail with a metal spare wheel cover as standard and a folding rear luggage rack. The single waist moulding now continued around the rear of the car below the window. The rear side windows were now openable on hinges, and there were semaphore trafficators embedded in the upper B-pillars. The front end had also been very noticeably redesigned, with the radiator now hidden behind a styled and painted cowl containing the grille.

The ARQ Ruby Saloon was the first of the new-look Sevens. This is a Standard model, with no front bumper. (Matthew Barker)

The bonnet sides now had vent flaps instead of louvres, there was a matching vent on each side of the scuttle, and the front wings had been redesigned to suit the new lines of the body.

The best-selling De Luxe models came with a Pytchley sunroof, but the Standard models had a solid roof with a smoker's vent. They also lacked bumpers, and had black-painted rather than silver grille slats. Where the De Luxe models had a fixed starting-handle, that on the Standard cars was removable (necessary because the absence of a front bumper would have made it a dangerous projection). Standard cars also had black headlamp shells (although the rims were chromed) and black-painted wheels. On both models, hide upholstery was standard at first, but was supplemented by cloth or moquette during 1935. A minor modification in May 1936 reduced draughts by adding trim panels over the interior vents.

The De Luxe model was initially priced at £120, and the Standard car at £112. In August 1935, both prices were increased, to £125 and £118 respectively.

The first Ruby or Type ARQ had square lower corners to its side windows.

TYPE AEK SPEEDY, 1934-1936

The EK Sports 75 took on a three-letter works code as the AEK in summer 1934 and, for public consumption, was renamed the Speedy. That name was doubtless intended to underline the greater performance than was available from the contemporary Nippy. Like the Nippy, the Speedy was also built with left-hand drive.

The bodies for all the EK and AEK models were built as a batch, and were taken from

The Speedy was an attractive-looking car, although the picture of the Brooklands banking in the background perhaps suggested a little too much.

stock as orders were received. There is some disagreement over when production ended, whether in 1935 or June 1936, but it is quite clear that the car was not a strong seller. A best guess is that around 60 were built. Some unused bodies were probably sold to Cooper's of Putney together with unused bodies for the AEB Nippy.

TYPE AAK OPEN ROAD TOURER, 1934-1936 (JULY 1934)

The AAK was the Tourer contemporary of the ARQ Ruby saloon, and took on many of that model's features, perhaps the most obvious being the radiator grille with its body-coloured cowling and the accompanying bonnet with ventilator flaps instead of louvres. The scuttle also had a vent on each side, and the front wings had been redesigned.

Otherwise, the body was very similar to that of the Type AH, with steel panels on an ash frame and doors that were once again square-shaped. The spare wheel was carried on the tail panel, and had no cover. Unlike the ARQ, however, the AAK did not have a low chassis frame but retained the high chassis of its predecessors.

The first of these Tourers was built in July 1934 with chassis number 198596, and the initial showroom price was £108. They remained in production until August 1936.

The high chassis was still used on the AAK Tourer, which made the car look less modern than some contemporary Seven models.

TYPE AC OR PEARL CABRIOLET, 1934-1936 (AUGUST 1934)

The first version of the Pearl Cabriolet was announced in August 1934 and was very much a derivative of the ARQ Ruby Saloon that was new at the same time. The first 200 cars had three crossbars to brace the body between the cantrails, but later examples only had two bars.

The roll-back fabric roof of course had its own crossbars that were permanently engaged with channels in the cantrails. It also provided three positions: closed, fully open, or half-open and secured just behind and above the rear window. These followed exactly the practice with larger and grander "three-position" Drophead Coupés. The roof also had external "pram irons" behind the rear side windows that tensioned the fabric.

The AC Pearl Cabriolet was priced at £128, and the last examples were built in December 1936. Some of the last cars were actually built on the new ARR Saloon chassis that had become available in August 1936.

The first version of the Pearl Cabriolet, the Type AC, had prominent landau irons at the rear.

TYPE APD OR OPAL TWO-SEATER, 1934-1935 (AUGUST 1934)

The Opal Two-seater had both the high chassis and the old-style radiator grille, but was still a good-looking caR.

Minor changes to the PD introduced in August 1934 were accompanied by two new names as the model became the Opal in Austin's new "jewel" range and gained a three-letter factory code as the APD in line with the latest policy. They were otherwise essentially the same as the PD types, with the tall chromed radiator shell at a time when other models were switching to the new cowled radiator, and the addition of semaphore trafficators mounted on the sides of the scuttle. The APD Two-seater remained in production until August 1935 and was priced at exactly £100; this made it £8 cheaper than the contemporary four-seat Open Road model.

The British Army also took quantities of the APD model, and there are more details of these in Chapter 6.

TYPE AVJ DELIVERY VAN, 1935-1937 (JANUARY 1935)

The more modern appearance of the August 1934 Ruby Saloon and Pearl Cabriolet was not carried over to the vans when the revised AVJ type became available in January 1935. Austin policy was still to use up stocks of components left over from earlier models on the vans, no doubt in the belief that light commercial buyers were not very concerned about the latest automotive fashions as long as their vehicles did what was expected of them. The AVJ vans remained in production until July 1937.

However, the AVJ was rather more than a mish-mash of old-stock parts. The van body itself was revised, gaining a flatter roof and narrower cab doors that left more body length ahead of the rear mudguard, while at the tail the underfloor-mounted spare wheel projected through shaped cut-outs at the bottoms of the doors to provide a certain amount of rear-end collision protection. There were side lights mounted on the wings, probably from the start of AVJ production in January 1935.

The AVJ also evolved during its production to keep up with changes made to other models of the Seven. Synchromesh was added to second gear in November 1935, and the three-bearing engine arrived during 1936, but the vans were always the last in line to gain the latest improvements and they therefore lagged a little behind the other Seven models. They were certainly the last Sevens to switch to the low frame, during 1937.

The Type AVJ Delivery Van had a flatter roof than its predecessors but still had the old style of radiator grille and the high frame.

TYPE APE OR OPAL TWO SEATER, 1935-1938 (JULY 1935)

The APE version of the Opal was introduced in July 1935 and brought to the Two-seater the new low frame, painted grille surround, bonnet with flap-type vents and valanced front wings of the ARR Ruby saloon. The tail was identical in shape to that of the earlier PD/APD. Once again, access to the stowage in the tail was through the passenger compartment.

Early examples of the APE had trafficators, mounted on the scuttle sides. By late 1935 they were flush-mounted behind the doors. These models also gained the three-bearing engine in June 1936. They were priced at £102 10s 0d in 1937; this went up to £112 towards the end of the year, but in July 1938 it was reduced again, to £108. The last APEs were built either at the end of 1938 or in February 1939.

The second version of the Opal, the APE, generally resembled the first and was one of the models that was not supplied with a front bumper as standard.

Early examples of the APE appear had trafficators mounted on the scuttle sides. By summer 1937 they had been relocated to sit flush behind the doors. This 1938 car has them in this last position. (Robin Lawton)

TYPE ARR NEW RUBY SALOON, 1936-1939 (AUGUST 1936)

The final Seven Saloon was the ARR type or New Ruby that was introduced in August 1936. Although very similar in appearance to the ARQ Ruby that had preceded it, the ARR in fact had a number of important differences.

Most important of these was the new three-bearing engine, as described above. The front brakes were now of Girling manufacture, still operated by rods; as the rear brakes remained unchanged, the models with this system are generally described as "semi-Girling" types.

Immediately obvious in this catalogue illustration of a New Ruby or Type ARR Saloon are the rounded lower corners to the side windows.

From May 1938, rod-operated full Girling rear brakes were fitted. Wheels still had the same 17in diameter, although now with larger chromed centre caps, and a 16in size was available on export models.

The New Ruby's body was most easily recognisable by its radiused window surrounds, which were introduced partly to prevent the cracking at waist level of the windscreen pillars that had become a problem on the ARQ bodies. The waist moulding had also been redesigned and no longer ran across the rear panel, and the windscreen had a little more rake to it than before. The rear side windows were now arranged to wind down into the bodywork, as the hinges on the earlier bodies had proved weak, but of course the intrusion of the wheelarch meant that the glass would not descend fully. The wings, too, had been revised with deeper curves at their trailing edges.

Both Standard and De Luxe versions of the car were available, as before, and with similar differences. The De Luxe car had bumpers front and rear, a fixed starting handle and a sliding sunroof; the Standard car had no sunroof, no bumpers, and a removable starting handle. In both cases, the centre section of the roof was trimmed in Rexine.

As always, Austin incorporated improvements as they became available. So from October 1936, there was a SilentBloc rubber mounting point for the torque tube. Two months later came the improved "hourglass" steering. Then in July 1938, the De Luxe models gained a new design of sliding steel sunroof, and lost the Rexine covering from the main roof panel.

The De Luxe and Standard models started out with prices of £125 and £118 respectively. In March 1937 the Standard model went up to £122, and then in July 1938 both prices increased, to £125 and £122. Production of the De Luxe models ended in January 1939 but the Standard models were still being built into February. With war by this time looking inevitable, the prices of remaining stocks were reduced in April 1939 to £125 for the De Luxe model and £122 for the Standard type.

TYPE AAL OPEN ROAD TOURER, 1936-1939 (AUGUST 1936)

The first low-frame Tourer to the Type AAL specification was built in July 1935, but it appears that the AAL did not replace the AAK on production until as late as August 1936. By this time, the three-bearing engine and 17in wheels were very much part of the standard Seven specification.

The Tourer body has been described as that of the ARQ Ruby saloon with the top cut off, and it shared the sloping radiator cowl and front apron; the windscreen glass was also hinged on its top rail. The spare wheel was once again mounted on the tail panel, which this time was outswept, and on the AAL it had a shaped metal cover panel like that on the contemporary saloon. There was also a luggage rack that folded into the wheel well when not in use. Later models had semaphore trafficators let into the sides of the body behind the doors.

As first introduced, the AAL Tourer was

The AAL was the last of the Seven Tourers, and was essentially a Ruby Saloon with the upper body removed. (Robin Lawton)

priced at £102 10s 0d, but that figure was increased to £115 later in 1937. Prices were then lowered again, first to £112 in July 1938 and then to £108 in April 1939. By that time, production had actually ended, the last AAL models being built in January 1939.

TYPE ACA PEARL CABRIOLET, 1937-1939 (JANUARY 1937)

The Cabriolet took a few months to catch up with changes made to the parent Saloon range. The ARR Ruby replaced the ARQ model from August 1936 but its Pearl equivalent, the ACA, did not arrive until January 1937.

Minor changes associated with the ARR models aside, this second version of the Pearl Cabriolet was immediately recognisable by larger rear side windows and the absence of "pram irons" on the folding hood behind them. The body had also been reinforced, and on these models there were no crossbars between the cantrails.

The ACA model was introduced at the same £128 as the AC type that it replaced, but in July 1938 the price was increased to £135. Towards the end of 1938, the cost was reduced again, to £129, and the last cars were built in January 1939.

The second version of the Pearl Cabriolet had a different hood arrangement, with no landau irons and no fixed bracing bars between the cantrails.

This 1938 example is shown with the hood closed. (Matthew Barker)

TYPE AVK DELIVERY VAN, 1937-1939 (JULY 1937)

The last new variant of the Austin Seven van was the AVK model that entered production in July 1937 and ended its run in August 1939. The final examples for the UK seem to have been built in March, and the very last ones went for export.

The AVK van had an updated appearance thanks to the restyled front end panels that had been introduced with the Ruby (ARQ) Saloon as long ago as August 1934. The radiator cowl was painted black to match the wings, and the semaphore trafficators were now mounted flush with the body rather than externally, just behind the cab doors. The AVK was also the only variant of the Delivery Van to be built on the low-frame chassis.

The AVK Delivery Van was distinguished by its painted windscreen header rail.

These steel-panelled vans had a Rexine roof covering that stopped short of the front, where a painted windscreen surround panel gave them a quite distinctive appearance. The spare wheel once again projected through cut-outs in the lower sections of the tail doors, and on these vans the petrol tank was mounted below it, with a filler low down on the left-hand side of the body. The floor level of the back body was raised up to give a flat load area. As was by now expected, only a driver's seat was supplied as standard, and when the optional passenger seat was not added, the van body had a load capacity of 55½ cu ft. In primer, the van cost £110, and Austin factory colours could be had at extra cost.

There were a few changes during the production run. Following developments on the mainstream Sevens, these vans took on the all-Girling braking system from October 1938.

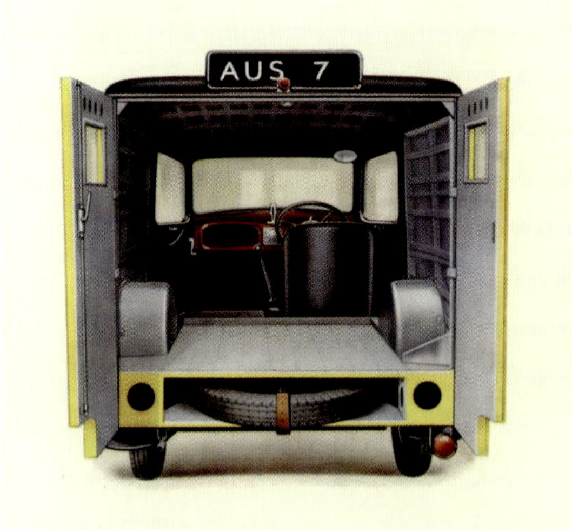

The AVK came without a passenger seat as standard, and also had no internal bulkhead.

Identification, 1934-1939

Austin Sevens built before July 1936 are usually identified by their Car Number, which is shown on the service plate. This is an oblong plate that is riveted to the scuttle.

Car Numbers consist of a sequence prefix that is the three-letter code for the model type (eg ARR), and each type has its own serial number sequence. Note that Car Numbers and Chassis Numbers did not match in this period, and that Engine Numbers also had their own separate sequence.

From July 1936, the system changed and the Car Number and Chassis Number were the same. This new system was introduced at 249701; the last Austin Seven built, in March 1939, was an AVH Delivery Van with number 291000.

No build records survive for cars from this period.

Production totals, 1934-1939

Below are the generally accepted annual production figures for the Austin Seven. Note that the 1934 figures are for the calendar-year and therefore contain models covered in the preceding Chapter as well as those introduced in mid-1934 and discussed in the present Chapter.

1934	22,685
1935	27,225
1936	24,523
1937	20,671
1938	8089
1939	656

Individual type totals for the 1934 and 1935 calendar-years were compiled by RJ Wyatt for his 1982 book, *Austin Seven – The Motor for the Million*. Wyatt was well aware that his figures were incomplete and in some cases were approximations, but they have generally been accepted as presenting a reasonably accurate guide. The figures for the 1934 calendar year repeat those shown in Chapter 4, with the addition of the Cabriolets that were built in the latter part of the year.

	1934	1935
Chassis	713	1392
Tourers	1449	1362
Saloons	2901	4343
De Luxe Saloons	13,638	15,864
Cabriolets	76	1052
Two-seaters	1015	735
Delivery Vans (Austin)	2380	1916

These individual totals once again show the overwhelming customer preference for Saloons with De Luxe equipment levels.

Technical Specifications, 1934-1939

Engine: Four-cylinder side-valve, 1934-36 – two main bearings, 1930-39 – three main bearings

Capacity: 747.5ccc

Bore x stroke: 56mm x 76mm

Induction: 1934-35: Zenith type 26VA carburettor; 1935-39: Zenith type 26

Power: 1934-36: 3bhp at 2400rpm;
1936-39: 17bhp at 2400rpm
21bhp at 4400rpm (Nippy),
23bhp at 4800rpm (Speedy)

Gearbox: Four-speed with reverse, Gear ratios – 4.37:1, 2.64:1, 1.66:1, 1.00:1; reverse 5.62:1
Synchromesh on 2nd, 3rd and 4th gears

Axle ratio: Standard 5.25:1 (to 1936) 5.125:1 (from 1936); Sports 5.65:1

Brakes: Drums all round, 7in x 1¼in. Coupled brakes (both handbrake and footbrake act on all four wheels). Full Girling brakes from July 1938.

Steering: Worm and wheel type

Front suspension: Beam axle with transverse leaf spring and radius arms

Rear suspension: Beam axle with quarter-elliptic leaf springs

Wheels and tyres: Wire wheels, 17in as standard, with black centres on standard models or Staybrite centres on others; large Staybrite centres from 1936; no locating dowels from July 1938. The 16in wire wheels optional on Sports models had Staybrite centres.
17 x 4.00 tyres Ruby and Pearl models,
19 x 3.50 tyres Open and Sports models,
16 x 4.75 tyres Export Ruby and Pearl; optional on Sports models from 1935
18 x 4.00 tyres Export Open and Sports models; low-chassis, Delivery Vans

Length: 119in/3023mm (typical)
126.5in/3213mm (AVJ Delivery Van)

Wheelbase: 81in/2057mm

Width: 46in/1168mm (typical)
53in/1346mm (AVJ Van

Front Track: 40in/1016mm

Rear Track: 43in/1092mm

Weight: 800lb approx (typical)

MILITARY SEVENS

Between 1929 and 1936, several hundred Austin Sevens were supplied to the British Army for reconnaissance duties; Bryan Purves (*The Austin Seven Source Book*) puts the total at 1262 cars. In 1937 a further quantity was built for the Indian Army.

There is surprisingly little information available about these models, but fortunately a small number have survived into preservation. Some examples were "civilianised" when sold off by the Army, and some of these have also survived in their modified form. All those for the British Army were delivered with all-over Deep Bronze Green paint, which was the standard "peacetime" livery for military vehicles. Interiors were black. Many were still in service during the early years of the Second World War.

The military variants had factory approval, and the special Mulliner-built variants were promoted with their own special catalogue.

Pictures of these models on active service are rare, and this one may well have been specially posed. In the early days, military vehicles carried standard civilian-style number plates.

1928 SCOUT CAR PROTOTYPES

Pioneering mechanised warfare theorist Lt Col Giffard Le Quesne Martel was co-opted onto the Army's Mechanical Warfare Board in March 1928, and it was not long before he was able to follow up his ideas for a light reconnaissance vehicle that could be attached to a larger mechanised force. In July that year, Austin received a letter requesting their assistance.

As David Fetcher explains in his book *Mechanised Force*, "Martel was commanding 17 Field Company RE, yet his mind, as ever, was considering wider matters. He managed to borrow two Austin Sevens from their manufacturers – or at least running chassis complete with bonnet, radiator and front mudguards, but precious little else in the way of bodywork. Both were fitted with crude wooden seats and a sort of pedestal on which a man could stand to get a better view. A stout plank beneath the chassis protected the sump and gearbox and rope slings hung down on each side. The cars carried a crew of two: driver and observer, armed only with their rifles. In these lightweight cars they could set out on scouting missions at considerable speed while remaining inconspicuous and quiet. Their task was to gather information, not fight for it.... [Martel] had the rope slings fitted so that the crew could manhandle their car bodily over ... obstacles [...]. In the event nothing resulted from this experiment, at least along the lines that Martel suggested, although the baby Austin was adopted as a liaison vehicle and, later, as a wireless car for many years."

Martel's idea for a stripped-down scout car based on the Seven was not followed up. Two soldiers here prove that the car was light enough to be manhandled if necessary.

To this description, Bryan Purves (*The Austin Seven Source Book*) adds that the minimal bodywork was made from aluminium sheet over an ash frame; that the spare wheel, tools, and an auxiliary petrol can were stowed in the rear; and that the modifications were carried out by 17 Field Workshops, which were of course under Martel's direct command.

1929-1930 MULLINER MILITARY SEVEN

Although Martel's idea of using the Seven as a scout car attached to mechanised units was not directly followed up, a first order from the military for scout cars was placed the following year. These were required to replace the motorcycles then in use for scouting duties by the Cavalry regiments. The choice probably fell on the Austin Seven because of its low cost and known reliability, but Austin themselves were either unable or unwilling to make the modifications that the Army wanted, and so the body contract was given to the coachbuilder Mulliners Ltd, of Bordesley Green in Birmingham. (There is more about this company in Chapter 7.) Early military photographs probably taken for record purposes show a car with the early scuttle-mounted headlamp configuration, and this may have been a prototype.

The first cars appear to have been delivered in March 1929. The chassis supplied to the military were essentially the standard production type of the time, equipped with uprated road springs and 4in wide Dunlop tyres on 19-inch wire wheels. They were specially fitted with a towing eye at the front and with a low-ratio final drive giving a 5.66:1 ratio. Early examples had tow hooks on the front axle, but later ones had lifting lugs (shaped like cotton reels) riveted to the wheel centres. The engine was again standard, but with a Zenith 22FZB (Mazak-bodied) carburettor, and on later deliveries with a larger oil sump as

well. Wings and running-boards changed to reflect changes on standard production, first in October 1929 and then again in January 1930.

The Mulliner bodies were steel-panelled two-seaters and had an angular tail with an access hatch low down on the vertical rear panel and an angled lid with quick-release clips for two rifles. There was a single door on the passenger's side, and the spare wheel was carried where the driver's door would have been. There was a shallow, one-piece windscreen and the frame of the simple folding hood was attached to the body sides behind the seats and ahead of the tail stowage box. The space behind the seats and within the body could be used for equipment stowage.

There were 158 of these cars, 118 being built in 1929 and 40 more in 1930. Two examples are known to survive.

This military record picture shows the 1928 prototype Mulliner Scout Car.

1929 GORDON ENGLAND WD MODEL

Two months after the Cavalry placed their order for Mulliner-bodied Sevens, an Army order was placed with Gordon England for 65 cars intended for surveillance and general duties. These were based on the Gordon England Cup model, a lightweight open two-seater introduced in August 1925 (see Chapter 10). They had heavy-duty road springs to increase ground clearance and low-ratio 5.66:1 rear axle gearing. Their 19-inch wire wheels had Dunlop heavy-duty tyres with a 3.5in width, and there was a lifting lug in the centre of each wheel.

1932 MULLINER SCOUT CAR

Austin clearly approved of the Mulliner conversion and actually produced a sales brochure that described it as "The Austin Seven Military Model" – although the brochure did not mention Mulliner's involvement. The model was available with either right-hand or left-hand drive, and with either the 75in wheelbase or the new 81in wheelbase. It came with "a weatherproof hood and side curtains, ample ground clearance, large tyres, plenty of locker space and complete equipment." In the case of left-hand

The special Mulliner military model had a squared-off tail and always carried its spare wheel alongside the driver.

drive models, the spare wheel was of course mounted alongside the driver on the left of the body.

One order was placed for a number of cars to be shipped to Egypt for desert use. A late cancellation resulted in them being sold off to the public in Britain. These cars had very similar bodies to the earlier Mulliner deliveries, modified to suit the longer wheelbase that had become standard on production, and with the addition of a double-skinned scuttle to keep heat off the petrol tank. There was a fixed windscreen, with a hand-operated wiper on the driver's side.

The chassis and front-end panels were again as used on contemporary production, although the engine was provided with a gear-driven water pump for more positive cooling. The wheels had a 19-inch diameter and 3-inch rim width, and were fitted with 19 x 4.00 Dunlop Fort block-pattern tyres and with lifting extensions like those on the later examples delivered to the British Army.

This catalogue picture illustrated the LHD model, with spare wheel again on the driver's side. The tail contained lidded lockers.

This Mulliner military Seven was pictured with the Duke of Gloucester at the wheel.

1932 MILITARY WIRELESS CAR

Austin clearly saw a future in making a military Seven of their own and had one ready during 1932. The British Army ordered a quantity as Wireless Cars; their role was much the same as the earlier reconnaissance models but with the added advantage that messages could be relayed back to headquarters more easily. The chassis was essentially to 1932 production standard but had a strengthened differential casing with 5.66:1 low-ratio gearing.

This Austin Seven wireless car is a 1932 model that has been preserved and is on display at the Royal Signals Museum. The aerial array is somewhat cumbersome but typical of the era. (Clive Barker)

The engine cooling arrangements were uprated with a gear-driven water pump and a large four-blade fan driven by twin belts. The wheels were once again 19-inch types with a 3-inch rim width, Dunlop Fort block-pattern tyres, and cotton-reel shaped lifting lugs riveted to their centres.

The body was an open two-seater with a squared-off rear that incorporated a drop-down tailgate, which carried the spare wheel. A high sill on each side probably added strength, and the rear-hinged doors had no external handles. The windscreen was fixed and sloped slightly to the rear, with a spotlight mounted on the driver's side pillar. It was mounted on a unique widened and squared-off scuttle that allowed a No.1 Wireless Set to be mounted in front of the operator. There was a simple folding hood on a frame secured just above the rear wheel arches, and each door had a detachable sidescreen. The hood reached to the

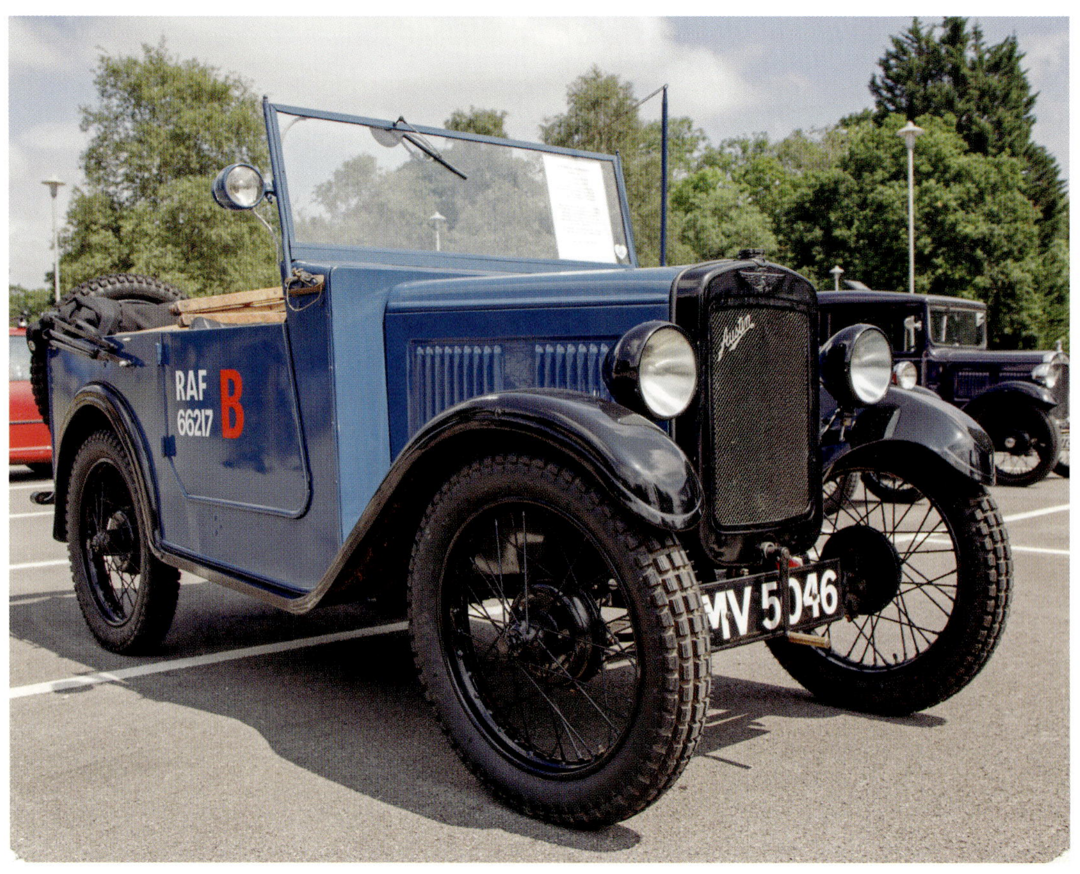

A 1932 RAF wireless car showing the widened and squared-off scuttle that allowed the wireless set to be mounted in front of the operator. (Matthew Barker)

tail of the body but its sloping rear panel could be rolled up to give access to the equipment stowage behind the seats, and the rear floor pan was extended forwards to provide a larger flat surface behind the seats.

The restored example that survives in the Royal Signals Museum at Blandford Forum is preserved complete with its wireless aerial array. The aerial was supported by a mast attached to the left side of the scuttle that was braced by wires; it cannot have been very quick for the two-man crew to erect.

1933 MILITARY TYPE PD

The British Army placed an order for a quantity of PD Two-seaters with minimal modifications, and deliveries to meet this began in November 1933. These cars were probably not intended for reconnaissance duties but rather for more general staff work.

The specification was that of the 1933 PD model with its gearbox incorporating synchromesh on the top two gears. A small number of modifications included uprated road springs all round, and a small towing eye at the front of the chassis. The wheels were initially the 19in size but some cars came with 17in and even 16in sizes, and from March 1933 the 17in wheels incorporated lifting lugs. Other special features were an inspection lamp socket on the dashboard, an off switch for the brake light, and semaphore trafficators mounted on the windscreen pillars. Some cars had a pair of U-shaped rifle clips on the transmission tunnel between the seats, and a lockable ammunition box under the tipping passenger seat.

1934-1936 MILITARY TOURER TYPE APD

The 1933 order was followed by more orders, and between July 1934 and (probably) October 1936 a large quantity of type APD Two-seaters were delivered to the British Army. The number has been estimated at 225. Confusingly, the Army called them Military Tourers. Though similar to the earlier PD types and retaining the older style of radiator shell, these had the contemporary Ruby style of dashboard and steering wheel. Most had green hoods, although some hoods were black. Some had the four-speed gearbox with two synchronised gears, and later deliveries had the type with three synchronised gears.

Special features differed from one contract to another, and no doubt depended on the intended use. Early deliveries had 19in wheels with 4in tyres; many later ones had 17in wheels; and some had 16in wheels with 5.25in Dunlop Trakgrip tyres. From December 1935, the 17in wheels had deeper rims and were spoked differently from earlier WD wheels; they also had lifting lugs riveted on their centres. Some cars had a water pump drive. Probably all had the inspection lamp socket on the dashboard and the off switch for the brake light, a towing eye on the front road spring centre mounting (later ones being longer), and "cotton-reel" lifting lugs riveted to the wheel centres. Some cars had the U-shaped rifle clips on the transmission tunnel between the seats, plus the ammunition box under the passenger seat. Some had no trafficators but a rifle cradle mounted vertically outside the body beside the windscreen on one side. Some carried medical panniers and a spare petrol can in the tail.

The British Army took a sizeable quantity of Type APD Two-seaters. The chassis number written on the original photograph suggests that this one was built in 1935.

APD Military Tourers being trimmed at Longbridge. Note the War Department boxes in the foreground.

1937 MILITARY TOURER TYPE PD

The last known order for military Austin Sevens was for a batch of 26 destined for Indian Cavalry units based on the North West Frontier of colonial India (today, the western frontier of Pakistan). These were delivered in April 1937 via an agency in Karachi.

These were adapted from the Two-seater production model of the time, with a high-frame chassis that had uprated road springs all round. There was a special final drive ratio, likely to have been the ultra-low 5.66:1 type, and the cooling system was uprated with a water pump and special radiator. Tyres were 5.25in Dunlop Trakgrips on 16in wheels.

The cars had no doors or sidescreens, although they did have a conventional folding roof. There were stowage clamps in the rear for medical panniers and an auxiliary petrol can, and some sources claim that the passenger seat was angled slightly towards the centre of the car.

Military Production totals

These figures were compiled by RJ Wyatt for his 1982 book, *Austin Seven – The Motor for the Million.* Wyatt was well aware that his figures were incomplete and in some cases were approximations, but they have generally been accepted as presenting a reasonably accurate guide.

No figures for Military models are available for the years 1936-1939.

1929	118
1930	40
1931	NIL
1932	127 (all Saloons)
1933	4 (all Two-seaters)
1934	141 (all Two-seaters)
1935	396 (all Two-seaters)

Military Contracts

The British military Sevens were purchased under a large number of separate contracts. Note that the list below also includes models described as "four-seaters", which were presumably four-seat Tourers. Some details still remain to be discovered.

The first two columns show the military contract number and its date, where known. The third column shows the quantity ordered. The fourth shows the military bonnet numbers (ie the serial number painted on the bonnet), and the fifth column contains remarks. Note that the comments on military record cards are sometimes rather cryptic!

Model type is Two-seater unless specified otherwise; some of the early contracts listed (pre-1932) probably relate to the Mulliner, Gordon England, and other purchases. "LP" in the contract number column indicates a Local Purchase; that is, a vehicle purchased directly by a military unit and not through the central purchasing system. There appear to have been some transfers between units, including the RASC (Royal Army Service Corps). BP in the Remarks column indicates that information comes from Bryan Purves' *The Austin Seven Source Book*.

I am grateful to military vehicle historian Geoff Fletcher for his help in compiling this table.

Contract	Date	Qty	Bonnet numbers	Remarks
V1866				BP. No further information.
V1942				BP. No further information.
V2103				BP. No further information.
V2198				BP. No further information.
V2223				BP. No further information.
V2243				BP. No further information.
V2323				BP. No further information.
V2499	10/06/33	24	M33468-M33491	BP says this contract was for 36 APD Tourers.
V2659		1	M33494	
V2570	01/01/33	66	M33505-M33578	BP says contract V2570 was for 110 APD Tourers.
	01/01/33	40	M33655-M33694	
		19	M33766-M33784	
LP		1	M33708	
V2611	19/03/34	1	M34000	Cost £88 0s 0d.
V2361		1	M34239	Four-seater.
V2653	31/07/34	114	M34414-M34527	APD models; £85 14s 9d each.
	31/07/34	22	M34532-M34553	APD models; £85 14s 9d each; numbered within the range of serials shown.
LP		1	M34736	
V2734	07/06/35	18	M35030-M35047	RASC; possibly numbered from M35040 and not as shown.
V2809	22/10/35?	19	M35246-M35264	Four-seater open; ex-RASC on 06/03/42.
V2734	07/06/35	204	M35316-M35519	Cost £83 17s 6d each.
V2816	12/35	253		BP lists this contract but gives no serial numbers.
V13326		14	M36215-M36228	Four-seaters.
V2980	05/08/36	16	M36273-M36288	First one probably numbered M36274 and not as shown; possibly only 13 within the range of numbers; ex-RASC.
		2	M36339-M36340	
		1	M36622	Described as "car".
V3082	21/06/37	5	M37175-M37179	Cost £99 19s 3d each; RASC.
	21/06/37	384	M377843-M378226	Delivered July-October; cost £99 19s 3d each; "allocated to 378231".
		1	M37736	Four-seater.
		2	M38379-M38380	Four-seaters.
		1	M39936	Four-seater.
V3349	03/10/38	22	M3811042-M3811063	Two-seater "Saloons".
V3348	29/10/38	18	M3912093-M3812110	
V3881		1	M3812111	Four-seater.
		1	M3812117	Four-seater.

GORDON ENGLAND, MULLINER AND SWALLOW

Special bodies by independent coachbuilders proliferated on the Seven from the middle of the 1920s, and of course Austin were only too happy to supply the bare chassis for the purpose. Some of these chassis were distinguished by a CH prefix in their numbers, although the practice may have been discontinued in 1927.

The majority of special bodies were built before 1930; the Depression played havoc with the coachbuilding industry generally, and those companies that survived tended to be much more cautious with their products during the following decade. The major players during this period of special coachbuilding were Gordon England, Mulliner, and Swallow, although many smaller firms also created designs for the Austin Seven. This Chapter focuses on the work of those three companies, and the following Chapter looks at the bodies offered by other independent companies.

GORDON ENGLAND

EC Gordon England had a background in aviation, having served as the works manager at the prestigious Bristol Aeroplane Co during the First World War. However, his interests took a turn towards motor racing, and in 1922, he and his father created the body for an Austin Seven, which went on to achieve remarkable success in various motorsport events. This achievement spurred England's decision to enter the motor bodywork business more seriously, leading to the establishment of a company in 1925 under his father's name, George England Ltd, located in Putney, SW London.

Despite his passion for competition, England primarily focused on developing innovative bodywork, drawing inspiration from aircraft engineering practices. Gordon England bodies were constructed with plywood panels built into box sections that was padded with cotton wadding and covered in Rexine fabric, and they sat on a rigid base frame that was mounted to the chassis at three points. The seats were mounted directly to the chassis, and this arrangement produced bodies that were not only light in weight but also "silent", in that they did not squeak and flex with the chassis.

Demand for Gordon England's designs soared, and his work caught the attention of Sir Herbert Austin, who was so impressed that he agreed to include Gordon England designs in the company's catalogue from 1926. As the business flourished, the company relocated to more spacious premises in Wembley in 1927, and by the following year, they were producing nearly 3000 bodies annually (not all for the Austin Seven). The Sports and Tourer types were accompanied by Delivery Van bodies, too.

In 1929, in preparation for going public, the company was restructured and became known as Gordon England (1929) Ltd. However, despite its ambitions for expansion, the company faced challenges as fabric bodies began losing popularity to the emerging all-metal body types. Unfortunately, the Great Depression further exacerbated their difficulties, ultimately leading to the closure of the Gordon England company in 1930.

BROOKLANDS AND SUPER SPORTS, 1924

The first Gordon England model to be sold was the Brooklands model of 1924. This came in three versions, as a Tourer or Sports for road use, or as a Super Sports for competition use.

The bodywork was a lightweight two-seater type with typical "speed" styling of the time that featured a sloped and pointed tail. It was framed in three-ply and panelled in aluminium. An outside exhaust with fashionable fishtail outlet was standard, and a windscreen, a hood, and wings were features of the road cars that cost extra on the Super Sports (and were readily detachable for competition). The Tourer cost £149 and the Sports £159, but both were built for looks rather than high performance.

The Super Sports was considerably more expensive at £265, a figure that was further inflated if the customer ordered the hood, windscreen, and wings. It was delivered as standard with a bright aluminium finish, and its two bucket seats were staggered, the co-driver's being set 9in further back than the driver's. Engine modifications included twin Zenith 30HK carburettors, a high-lift camshaft, a high-compression cylinder head, special valves with double springs, and special pistons. The cars had a streamlined undershield and a special fairing over the front axle, a tall 4.5:1 axle ratio, and Hartford shock absorbers on all four wheels.

The Super Sports was supplied with a

In full racing trim, the Gordon England Super Sportswas guaranteed to reach 80mph. With wings, windscreen and hood in place, the top speed was nearer 65mph.

The cars had a streamlined undershield and a special fairing over the front axle.

The Austin Seven "Brooklands" Super-Sports Model

Guaranteed . . . 80 m.p.h.

To meet the demand for a small two-seater racing car, the 7h.p. "Brooklands" Super-Sports Model has been produced. The engine capacity is 747.5 cc. (56 mm.×76 mm.), so that it can be entered for any sporting events of the 750 cc. class. It has already proved its merits at Brooklands racing track, and at hill climbs. The first cost and maintenance are extremely low for a car capable of a speed of 80 m.p.h. on the track. *Each car will be sold with a Brooklands Certificate of 80 m.p.h. before delivery.*

certificate guaranteeing an 80mph top speed, although later this was reduced to 75mph (and the certificates then pointed out that only 65mph was available with windscreen, hood and wings in place). By 1926, a Brooklands Super Sports was very expensive, at £505 with full equipment.

Production quantities are not known, but the total for all versions of the Gordon England Brooklands has been estimated at 350-400. When production ended in late 1926, roughly three or four cars were being built each week.

Guaranteed to attain 80mph – or at least, the early ones were.

CUP MODEL, 1925-1929

Within a year of the Brooklands model's introduction, the Gordon England company had followed up with a new model called the Cup. Introduced in August 1925, this was a light and sporting road-going two-seater with long tapering front wings and short running-boards. It always had a Triplex safety windscreen and fabric-covered plywood panels, and could be had optionally with the tuned "Brooklands" engine from the competition model of that name. While the new works at Putney became operational, early bodies were

The Gordon England Cup model was an attractive road car that benefited from the reputation of the more expensive Brooklands type. (Clive Barker)

built by Weymann (who had bought the old Cunard coachworks, also in Putney).

The Cup model sold well. Quantities have been estimated at six a week before 1928; in 1928 there were then 908 (rather more than 17 a week on average), and a further 494 were built before production ended in March 1929. The model evolved to some extent during its production run of just over three and a half years. From early 1926 the bonnet sides gained louvres, and during 1928 the door depth was reduced to improve body rigidity. When first introduced, it cost £185, but by October 1926 the price had fallen to £150, and from September 1928 the Cup model cost £140.

Rear three-quarter view of this "as-found" example shows the neat tail treatment.

GORDON ENGLAND SILENT SALOON, 1926-1928

The announcement of the Gordon England Silent Saloon came in December 1925 with production commencing in the spring of 1926. Austin did not have a Saloon model of their own yet, but the success of the Gordon England type was certainly a factor in prompting them to develop one. In the mean time, Herbert Austin was sufficiently impressed with the Silent Saloon to include both this and the Cup model in his own company's sales material. The body was built with the familiar plywood panelling and fabric covering, and used wings supplied by Austin. Impressively, the Silent Saloon was actually lighter than the contemporary Seven Tourer, although at £170 it was considerably more expensive. The early cars had no windscreen wiper or side lights, and had plain bonnet sides; a vacuum wiper, side lights, and louvred bonnet sides arrived later in 1926.

A further developed Silent Saloon was introduced alongside Austin's own Type R Saloon, which had an aluminium-panelled body. This now used the chassis of the latest Type D (or AD) Tourer, and was actually built by Gordon England under contract to Austin,

This Gordon England Saloon shows the clean lines for which the model was known.

using the company's familiar lightweight construction methods. Its fabric-covered body was distinguished by contrasting black upper panels.

Sir Herbert Austin knew exactly what he was doing, of course, and the Gordon England Saloon was always considerably more expensive than Austin's own offering of its time. On its introduction it cost £210; the price quickly dropped to £195 a month later, and then became gradually lower. In September 1927 it was £170 and by September 1928 £160 – which was still £25 more than the Austin metal-panelled offering.

EARLY DELIVERY VANS, 1927-1928

This Gordon England Delivery Van dates from 1927 and is thought to be the prototype.

A little while after the Fabric Saloon made its appearance, Gordon England announced a Delivery Van on the Seven chassis – an alternative to the Startin-built van built to Austin's own design. Although the Austin Motor Company supplied the chassis for bodying to George England Ltd, the Delivery Vans were not built under contract to Austin but as an independent venture.

Inevitably, the Gordon England vans had a number of differences from the Austin-designed Startin type. They were initially based on England's own Fabric Saloon structure and always had a nickel-plated radiator shell. The earliest examples may have been based on the Fabric Saloon's scuttle and one-piece fixed windscreen, although the windscreen was later modified to open outwards early and a single wiper was added at the same time.

The Gordon England vans had no door on the passenger side, where the space was used to mount the spare wheel, so freeing up some room in the van body. On the driver's side, a full-height door incorporated a glazed window. The roof sloped only towards the front, there was no bulkhead between the cab and the load area, and the tail doors had oval windows.

5CWT DELIVERY VAN, 1928-1929

A second type of van came from Gordon England in March 1928, this time designed to outdo its rivals by being designed to carry a much arger load of 5 cwt (660 lb, 299kg) – or twice as much as a Startin van. The body used the patented Gordon England lightweight wooden structure with a three-point mounting to the chassis, and that must have played its part in permitting an increased payload. The

The Gordon England vans had the spare wheel mounted externally on the passenger's side. This was a batch of 1929 vans for the Dunlop rubber company.

floor and driver's seat were mounted directly to the chassis, independently of the body structure, and the fabric skin panels could be cellulose-finished in one of four colours.

Like the earlier Gordon England vans, the 5cwt types had the spare wheel mounted on the kerb side so that it was not possible to have a passenger door, and there was a single rear door to the load area. These vans had the short bonnet of contemporary production Sevens, together with modified Austin wings and custom-made running-boards. Records show that 101 examples of this van were made.

A further-developed version of this van was available for 1929, differing in its use of the Type AD bonnet and scuttle panels. The vans remained available as late as October 1929 but their production ceased along with all other bodybuilding work when the Gordon England company finally closed its doors in 1930. Production quantities for these later vans can only be guesswork.

SUNSHINE SALOON, 1928-1929

More new Saloon models followed. February 1928 brought the Gordon England Sunshine Saloon, which had a roll-back roof panel made of black duck material. When opened, the "sunshine" panel rested in a roll on a small platform at the rear of the roof, while cross-bracing in the aperture maintained body rigidity at all times. A characteristic of these models was a small half-moon-shaped auxiliary petrol tank mounted low down on the driver's side front wing. Some were even fitted with a crude heater that was warmed by the exhaust pipe. The first cars cost £170, which fell to £165 by 1929.

The roof has been rolled back on this 1928 Gordon England Sunshine Saloon, and the fabric panelling gives an accurate representation of the way these cars looked when new. (Clive Barker)

The cross-bracing that maintained body rigidity without a fixed roof is clear in this picture of the Sunshine Saloon.

WEMBLEY SALOON, 1928-1929

The Gordon England Wembley Saloon had a much more sporting appearance than earlier Saloon models. This is a 1929 model. (Clive Barker)

The second new Saloon from Gordon England in 1928 was called the Wembley after the location of the new Gordon England works. It was an interesting attempt to add some sporting style to a Saloon body. The model was distinguished by a stylish curve to the upper rear panels, and had an external luggage boot with access only from inside the car, plus a ventilator (or "smoker's light") on the rear of the roof.

Early models had side lights on the wings but these were deleted when larger Lucas headlamps were fitted in 1929. A one-shot lubrication system was available as an option, and became standard from March 1929 when the model was also fitted with a sliding roof. Small circular vents were added to the scuttle sides at the same time, and there were a few minor trim changes as well. The Wembley saloon cost £160 initially, and later £165 with its improved equipment. Around 1000 examples are thought to have been made.

Those curved upper rear panels add to the sporting feel of the Wembley. (Clive Barker)

STADIUM TWO-SEATER, 1928-1929

The last new Gordon England body for the Seven was the Stadium Two-Seater, which took over from the Cup model during 1928. This time, the neat two-seater body had sheet metal panels, although they were still mounted on the patented three-point frame and were still covered with padded fabric. There was a tapered tail that contained the spare wheel, and the steering column was raked to allow lower lines, while the wings and running-boards were modified Austin types. The engine was a standard production type. Like the Wembley, the Stadium was available with the Tecalemit central chassis lubrication system.

Before the end of the year, the Stadium was modified with a higher tail and deeper rear wings, and also gained external door handles. In late 1929, the rounded lower corners of the doors gave way to angular types, and at about the same time the appearance of some aluminium-panelled bodies suggested that Gordon England designs were about to move on. The Stadium Sports cost £155 when first announced, but by March 1929 was priced at £140.

The Stadium Two-Seater took over from the Gordon England Cup during 1928.

The Stadium's neat, tapered tail contained the spare wheel.

MULLINER

The Mulliner company that was contracted to build bodywork on Austin chassis during the 1920s should not be confused with either of the other two British coachbuilders of that name – Arthur Mulliner of Northampton and HJ Mulliner of London. All three did have family links in the distant past, but by the early 20th century Mulliners Ltd of Bordesley Green, Birmingham was a fully independent company.

Between 1913 and 1924, Mulliners were fully committed to building bodies for Calthorpe, but when that company went under in 1924, its Managing Director, Louis Antweiler, bought the Mulliners coachbuilding business. He pursued a policy of contract bodybuilding, although Mulliners also did some bespoke work. By this time, the company had taken out a licence to use the Weymann patent coachwork with its fabric panelling and flexible framework joints, and most if not all of its work before 1932 depended on this.

Nevertheless, Mulliners' Works Manager found a way of circumventing the Weymann patents by using Irish linen instead of steel plates to create the flexible joints. It was a great idea that must have saved the company a considerable sum in licence fees, but it unfortunately backfired in the longer run, because the linen absorbed moisture and that led to the premature demise of many Mulliner bodies.

As a company dependent on contract work, Mulliners must have been delighted to secure a major contract from Austin in 1927 to provide special coachwork for the Seven. Company founder Herbert Hall Mulliner had known Herbert Austin from the latter's time at Wolseley in 1895-1896, and this may have played as much a part in the arrangements as did the geographical proximity of the two companies. The Seven was not the only Austin for which Mulliners built special coachwork, either: the company also provided bodies for the 12/4 chassis.

Mulliners produced three basic body types for the Austin Seven's civilian customers between 1927 and 1931. Mulliner used a standard Austin engine/chassis, floor pan, bonnet, wings, running boards, dashboard, fuel tank and bulkhead for the saloons. Sports models did not used the Austin wings or running boards and used a cut down bulkhead. They used a bonnet of similar design to the standard version but somewhat longer. There were Coupés, Saloons and Sports models, all with Weymann-style bodies; and on top of this there was, briefly, a fabric-bodied van with the grand-sounding title of Traveller's Brougham. Finally, Mulliners built a number of special bodies on Seven chassis for the British Army in 1929-1930, and some more in 1932 for use in Egypt. All these had metal-panelled bodies rather than fabric-panelled types, and they are discussed in more detail in Chapter 6.

The military contracts may well have been granted to Mulliners on the recommendation of the Austin company, which certainly endorsed the body maker's work. However, the major relationship between Mulliners and Austin seems to have ended in 1931, although there is one 1932 long-chassis Mulliner Sports still in existence. Fabric bodies had gone out of fashion. Austin was also by this time able to meet all the orders for the Seven that it received without needing to rely on outside body building capacity.

MULLINER FABRIC SALOON, 1927-1929

Austin already had a Fabric Saloon in production. However, fabric Saloons were fashionable in this period, and there was no chance that the Austin body works could keep up with demand. It therefore made sense to allow Mulliners to build their own; Austin of course still made a profit by selling the chassis. An all-black car introduced the new Mulliner Fabric Saloon at Olympia in October 1927. In this case, the production four-piece bonnet was retained, but Mulliners added their own style of circular ventilator to each side of the scuttle. The doors hinged at the front and were a rectangular shape with winding windows, while the rear windows incorporated a sliding section. The rear quarter carried stylish dummy

The Mulliner Fabric Saloon picked up on the fashion for dummy landau irons as well as that for fabric panels. (Simon Clay)

landau irons. All the skin panels were made from Rexine. As on the contemporary Mulliner Coupé, the earliest cars had scuttle-mounted headlamps and a split windscreen, but by 1928 there was a single-pane screen that was hinged at the top, and for that year the headlamps were relocated on the front wings.

These early Fabric Saloons cost £135 or, with the Triplex safety glass that made them De Luxe models, they cost £146.

Mulliners continued to offer the same basic Fabric Saloon design for the 1929 season, but from September 1928 added a sliding roof, as on the contemporary Coupé. With this, the model became a Sunshine Saloon and sold strongly: a production figure of 2868 examples is quoted. The cars were initially priced at £150 or, with Triplex safety glass, £160. However, during 1929 these prices were reduced to £140 and £150 respectively.

This 1929 Fabric Saloon example features the company's distinctive round scuttle vents and the sliding roof that arrived September 1928. (Simon Clay)

THE FIRST COUPÉ, 1927-1929

The first Mulliner Coupé body for the Seven was a neat enough two-seater with front-hinged doors and a neatly curved projecting luggage boot. This had external access through a large hinged lid. It was probably introduced at the same time as the Mulliner Fabric Saloon in October 1927, and the earliest models therefore had the scuttle-mounted headlamps that were standard on Sevens at the time. It also had a split windscreen, but by 1928 Mulliners were fitting a single-pane screen that was hinged at the top, and during that year the headlamps moved to the front wings because Austin was now supplying them like that.

These early-model Mulliner Coupés were available for around two years until autumn 1929, but they were not a great success: only seven are believed to have been made. In 1928, they were priced at £140 (or £150 with Triplex safety glass), and in 1929 they cost £160 plus £5 extra if a sliding roof was fitted.

These shots are of one of just two known survivors of the Mulliner Coupé, a most attractive body that in this case dates from 1929. (Matthew Barker, Clive Barker)

MULLINER TRAVELLER'S BROUGHAM, 1927-1929

The key features of the Mulliner Traveller's Brougham can be seen here: the rear body sides had no windows and the tail panel had a flap to give access to the load area.

Mulliners' third Austin Seven model in 1927 was in effect a fabric-bodied van, although instead of tail doors like those on the Delivery Vans by Startins and Gordon England, it had a half-height hatch that was hinged at roof level. This allowed the company to use the body structure of their Fabric Saloon and to mount the spare wheel on the tail panel below the hatch. Making a virtue out of necessity, Mulliners gave this model the rather grand title of Traveller's Brougham.

The £135 price of this new entry made clear that it was intended to undercut the Startins van (and later the Gordon England type as well), although a De Luxe model with Triplex safety glass was also available at £146. Like its competitors, it was rated to carry a 2½ cwt (280 lb, 127kg) load.

Like the parent Fabric Saloon, the van body was built using the Weymann principles. The Saloon's rear side windows were replaced by wrap-around quarter-panels, and three colours were available, with contrasting black wings, running-boards and radiator shell. A fourth colour was added in 1929. Early models were built on chassis that were supplied with headlamps on the scuttle, but from early 1928 they were relocated on the wings when Austin themselves made the change. Of note is that Austin gave some support to the Traveller's Brougham, by listing it in a November 1928 catalogue of models called Austin Models and Weymann Bodies.

SPORTS MODELS, 1928-1932

Mulliners completed their Austin Seven offerings with a Sports model a year after embarking on production of their Coupé and Fabric Saloon types. Availability probably began in October 1928, and the new model was advertised a month later along with its cousins in the sales brochure mentioned above.

The first Sports model was a neat and quite pert-looking design, matching a fairly square-rigged central section with rear-hinged doors to a boat-tail that had a small access hatch on top. The angled leading and trailing edges of the doors took some of the squareness away, and the front edge matched the angle of the raked windscreen, which was fixed in place. There were Mulliner's trademark circular vents in the scuttle, and sidelights mounted on the crowns of the front wings. The folding roof had external landau irons.

The Sports body was extensively redesigned a year later in October 1929, and now featured a pointed tail and fashionable cycle-type wings. Louvred panels below the body sides were another fashionable feature and helped make the car look lower. There was a vee-shaped windscreen with a hinged wind deflector at each end, and the front end was adorned with streamlined dumb-iron covers. This version of the Mulliner Sports cost £150 in 1929 and 1930, and was reduced to £140 in 1931.

The final version of the Mulliner Sports was introduced in November 1931, by which time it was clear that the public no longer wanted fabric-panelled bodies. It was no doubt as a result of this that its ash body frame was panelled in aluminium. It is not clear how many of these bodies were made.

The louvred panel alongside the chassis of this 1929 Mulliner Sports was a "fast-car" cue of the time, and the combination of a painted metal bonnet with fabric panels was quite common as well. (Clive Barker)

The Mulliner Sports evolved with the years. This 1932 car was one of the last built and still exists today. (Mike Tebbett)

MILITARY TOURERS, 1929-1930

From March 1929, Mulliners also secured a contract to supply special steel-panelled two-seater bodies on Austin Seven chassis for military use. The contract lasted into 1930. There is more about these special models in the previous chapter.

SECOND COUPÉ DESIGN, 1929-1931

A second design of Coupé by Mulliners was introduced at the Olympia Motor Show in October 1929. This was a more deliberately sporty-looking body, with a redesigned roofline and tail allied to a more raked windscreen and, thanks to its standard sliding roof, it was marketed as a Sunshine Coupé.

Taking its cue probably from the latest Swallow bodies for the Seven, the 1929 Coupé had a streamlined dumb-iron cover below the radiator. Mulliners had also chosen to provide their own design of bonnet, which nevertheless mated with the standard scuttle and radiator, and the fabric skin panels were delivered in two-tone, with those above the waistline matching the colour of the paint used on the wings.

This second Coupé design had longer rear doors than the first, hinged at the rear and with an angled leading edge which added to the slightly rakish sporting demeanour. Their disadvantage was that they extended over the rear wheelarch so that there was insufficient room for a drop-glass, and the windows were consequently sliding types. A second backward step was that the boot was no longer accessible from outside, but only from inside the car by tilting the seat back forwards. The price of these Coupés was probably the same £165 established earlier in 1929 for the earlier cars when fitted with a sliding roof.

LATER SALOON, 1929-1930

Along with the Coupé, the Mulliner Saloon was quite extensively redesigned in 1929 for its third year of availability. The body became wider and more curvaceous, and the doors were now rear-hinged. The dummy landau irons disappeared, standard letter-box scuttle vents replaced the coachbuilder's own round type – all changes that were perhaps the result of an attempt to reduce costs.

A sliding sunroof was a standard feature, as was a large glass visor mounted above the hinged windscreen. There was a stylish dumb-iron cover below the radiator, as on the other Mulliner-bodied Sevens announced at the Olympia Show in October 1929, and the interior was also given a more luxurious feel with a mahogany dash panel applied over the standard Austin type. They were trimmed in leather or Bedford Cord. These Fabric Saloons cost the same £140 as their predecessors.

The bottom half of this 1930 Mulliner Saloon was panelled in alloy, the top half was covered in fabric. (Mike Tebbett)

SWALLOW

Swallow started life in Blackpool as a maker of motorcycle sidecars. Owner William Walmsley partnered with William Lyons in 1922, and from 1926 the company also turned to car body manufacture. A year later, Swallow built its first body on an Austin Seven chassis, and this was a huge success. Streamlined production processes increased output, and demand, propelled by a major contract with Henlys in London, forced the company to find new premises in Coventry in late 1928. Here, Swallow built its first cars under the SS name in 1931, and later went on to become the Jaguar car company.

SWALLOW TWO-SEATER, 1927-1930

A first Austin Seven Swallow prototype was built in 1926, and production models became available in May 1927. They were always built on standard Seven chassis with nothing more radical than a more steeply raked steering column and a heavily-cowled radiator grille. The first cars wore only Austin badges, although the Austin Swallow name was added to the grille in September 1927. The first cars were open Two-seater models with a folding hood, but in 1928 a detachable aluminium roof became available as an alternative. Cars could then be ordered with either or both roof types.

These first Austin Swallow bodies had aluminium panels on an ash frame, a wasp tail and cycle wings; the wings were later revised with a more domed shape. Their style deliberately imitated that of more expensive coachbuilt cars, and they were always finished with bright two-tone paint schemes that were perfectly in harmony with the atmosphere of

The early Swallow two-seaters had an undeniable rightness of line, and bright two-colour paintwork made them stand out among special bodies from other manufacturers. *(Clive Barker)*

the 1920s. The 1927 cars were always Cream with wings and wheels contrasting in Dark Crimson Lake, but other options became available later. The 1927 price was £175, and the detachable hardtop cost an extra £10 when it became available; a car delivered with both tops cost £195. In 1929, prices dropped to £170 10s 0d for the open model, £180 10s 0d for the hardtop, and £185 10s 0d when both tops were supplied.

The two-seater still looked good with the hood raised. (Matthew Barker)

SWALLOW SALOON, 1928-1930

From the time of the Olympia Show in October 1928 there was a companion Saloon model – and Swallow made the same design available for Fiat, Standard and Swift chassis as well. Again aluminium-panelled over an ash frame, the Saloon had a positively exuberant appearance that was once again aided by bright two-tone colour schemes, now with a distinctive pen-nib shape on the bonnet top panels and a black leatherette roof covering. The wings and running-boards were steel, and the curved back panel and vee screen under a slightly peaked roof gave the Swallow an unmistakeable shape.

This Swallow Mk I Saloon shows the two-colour paint scheme with its "pen nib" on the bonnet and the ship-type scuttle ventilators that were briefly fashionable. (Clive Barker)

There were production changes, of course, as Swallow redesigned the roof structure so that a sunshine roof could be accommodated (at extra cost), added a footwell for rear-seat passengers and, from mid-1929, changed from a nickel-plated radiator shell to a chromed one. The earliest Austin Swallow Saloons cost £185, a figure that rose to £187 10s 0d in 1929.

MK II MODELS, 1930-1932

The Olympia Show in October 1930 brought Mk II versions of both models. There was no reason to change either the Swallow approach or the basic body shapes, but subtle changes were made to tidy up the original designs. The heavy radiator cowl gave way to a less bulbous one with a vertical centre bar, and both models gained front and rear bumpers. Inside the Saloon, individual front seats replaced the earlier bench. Prices went up in the darkest days of 1931 but fell again afterwards. The Mk II Sports was introduced at £165, went up to £170 10s 0d, and then dropped to £150 in 1932. As a hardtop, it was initially £175, increased to £180 10s 0d, and then fell to £165. With both roofs, the car was initially £185 10s 0d. The Saloons started at £187 10s 0d but were down at £164 by October 1931, the optional sunshine roof adding £5 to the cost.

The last of the Swallow-bodied Austin Sevens was built in October 1932. Unfortunately, no reliable production figures survive, but the relatively high survival rate of the cars themselves is a good indicator of how popular they were.

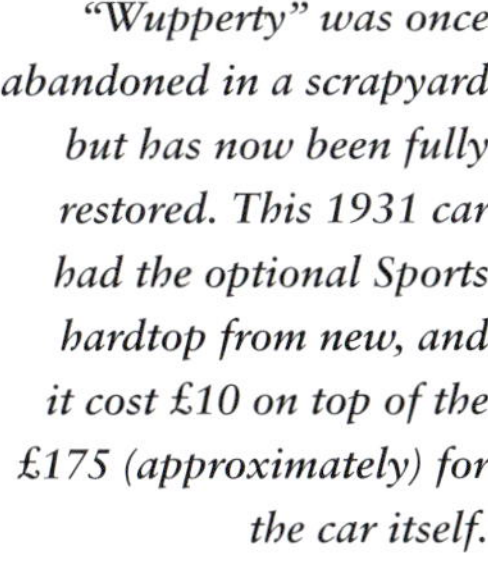

"Wupperty" was once abandoned in a scrapyard but has now been fully restored. This 1931 car had the optional Sports hardtop from new, and it cost £10 on top of the £175 (approximately) for the car itself.

A redesigned grille with a vertical bar makes clear that this 1931 car is a Mk II Swallow. (Clive Barker)

SPECIAL BODIES

In addition to the three major producers of special bodies for the Austin Seven that are covered in the preceding Chapter, many smaller independents tried their hand at building special coachwork on Seven chassis. Some of them, such as Martin Walter, may have built only a single body on the Seven, either to meet a customer's order or because the prototype they advertised so proudly may have attracted no interest. Probably not many of the smaller companies achieved a total production as high as 50 bodies. It may also be that some of the smaller companies are missing from the catalogue that follows in this Chapter for the simple reason that their work left no trace in contemporary magazines or in the shape of surviving cars.

Among these independent specialists, there were some who also offered performance tuning. Favourite methods of achieving high performance were to add a supercharger (typically a Cozette type, as used by the factory's own Super Sports model) or to fit an LAP overhead valve conversion. This came from LAP Engineering, of Kilburn in north west London. The company's Technical Director was Anthony Lago, who later became known for the Talbot Lago sports and racing cars. LAP offered several OHV conversions, for less expensive cars such as the Morris Cowley, Morris Oxford, MG Sports, and Austin 12hp. The conversion for the Austin Seven ingeniously used the original valve passages and ports for the pushrods that the overhead-valve cylinder head required, and was priced at £25. Its main benefit seems to have been to torque, although there were also minor improvements to top end power.

As was the case with chassis supplied to the coachbuilders covered in the previous Chapter, some of those supplied to the ones catalogued here were distinguished by a CH prefix in their numbers.

A car with a LAP overhead valve conversion. (Matthew Barker)

ABBOTT

ED Abbott had been the London sales representative of coachbuilder Page & Hunt, and when that company failed in 1929 he took over its premises and assets at Wrecclesham near Farnham, and formed a new company under his own name.

It was actually Page & Hunt who developed the first designs for the Austin Seven in 1928. They built 19 bodies for the Seven that year but, after this initial flurry of interest, demand dropped off sharply and only nine more were built – four in 1929, four in 1930, and a final example in 1932. Most of these later bodies really were built by Abbott, but for convenience all the bodies from the Farnham concern have historically been grouped together as Abbott products. The coachbuilder's records survive, and allow all these cars to be accurately identified and dated.

The earliest design was a Fixed-head Coupé with a fabric-panelled body, of which the first examples were built in February 1928. These two-seaters had a large boot with a hinged lid, and the spare wheel was thoughtfully mounted high up so that it could be removed without disturbing luggage. A walnut dashboard and mahogany running-boards on most cars added an air of luxury. Abbott made their own bonnets and wings, and there were some variations of design. The last of 22 examples was built in 1932.

The first of three Drophead Coupés was built in May 1928, its body design based on the fixed-head. Two more were made, one in 1928 and the second in 1929. A single Landaulet body – most unusual on a car of this size and class – was built with aluminium panels in June 1928, and the last new body was a Saloon that appeared in August 1928. Just two of these were built, the second in 1930 being fitted with a special folding head.

AEW

AEW was AE Wright Ltd of Alexandra Park in North London, a small coachbuilder that specialised in low-cut, sporting bodies for the smaller chassis in the 1930s. The company's work on the Austin Seven was done at a time when most other coachbuilders had long since stopped designing for the model, and may well have been prompted by a demand for similar bodies on the Wolseley Hornet Special chassis of the time. AEW offered engine tuning along with coachwork, and their final model in 1935 could be ordered with a supercharged engine.

AEW's earliest body for the Seven was in January 1933, and was an aluminium-panelled two-seater Sports that typified what would come later. The body was low-slung and rakish, with cutaway doors and a fold-flat windscreen. Cycle wings, louvred panels alongside the chassis frame, a spotlight on the windscreen pillar, and headlamps mounted as close as possible to the front of the car were all contemporary sporting cues. However, there was a degree of practicality as well in the large square-rigged tail that had an access hatch on its top surface and carried the spare wheel externally. The basic cost of the AEW Sports was £135, which was increased during 1934 to £139 10s 0d; however, some bodies incorporated individual customer preferences, such as wing designs, which would have inflated these figures.

A four-seater version of the same design was first built in February 1933, with the large tail being re-employed for the extra two seats.

Late AEW models were based on a modified 65 chassis, with either the 75 engine or a supercharged type. This advertisement dates from 1936.

Unfortunately, the larger folding hood tended to unbalance the design when erected. These cars cost £10 more than the two-seaters, with the same price differential being maintained after costs increased during 1934.

AEW moved on to base a new design on the type EB or 65 with its lowered chassis in October 1933. This was prettier than their earlier Sports model, now with swept wings, fashionable humps on the scuttle, and a slightly shorter tail that still had a top hatch for access. The external spare tyre had a neat metal cover that left the spokes of the wheel exposed, and what AEW called the Speed 65 came with a Burgess straight-through silencer to add a little extra performance. It cost £179 10s 0d, rising in 1935 to £185 10s 0d.

Then from August 1935 there was a further developed Sports model with similar bodywork but now with Austin's own 75 Speedy engine in the 65 chassis with a bowed front axle and other modifications. This was known as the K1 model and cost £185 10s 0d. As an alternative, this could be fitted with a supercharged engine that AEW claimed gave an 80mph top speed. In this guise, the car was known as a Z1 model and cost £205 10s 0d. Some late examples of these cars had a special radiator shell with the AEW logo in place of the Austin logo, but there may not have been many, as AEW closed down in 1936. One expert has suggested that the company may have built as many as 200 bodies for the Seven in all.

ALPE AND SAUNDERS

The only known body on a Seven by Alpe and Saunders was this 1928 three-quarter coupé.

The Alpe and Saunders company was established in London's Mayfair district in October 1925, but there is little information available about its early coachbuilding activities. The likelihood is that it acted as a broker and sub-contracted the actual building of bodies to other London firms. By the 1930s it was specialising in the hearses for which it is best known.

The company put its name to one known body on the Austin Seven chassis, a rather unattractive three-quarter coupé that cost £164 in 1928.

ARC

ARC Manufacturing of Hyde in Cheshire offered what they called a Drophead Coupette on the Seven chassis in 1927. "Coupette" was not a standard coachbuilding term, but was presumably intended to denote a little Coupé. This was an aluminium-panelled two-seater with a rather angular tail that provided luggage accommodation; access was gained by tilting the seats forward.

The car was priced at £175 in 1927 and was reduced to £160 in 1928. Production numbers are not known.

ARMSTRONG

This company was based in Shepherd's Bush, west London, and is known to have built at least one body on an Alvis chassis in 1929 as well as the Austin Seven Tourer that it offered in 1930.

The cycle-winged body provided two seats and had a twin-bladed rear bumper, but its most obvious characteristic was a bulbous luggage boot that stood several inches above the waistline. There is no information available about production quantities or prices.

ARROW

The first Arrow body for the Austin Seven was a coupé that was built in 1929 by the short-lived Compton Sons & Terry in Merton, SW London. Its designer was Arthur P Compton, who had formerly been with the Jarvis coachworks, and in late 1929 he set up in business on his own and took the Arrow name and design with him. Arrow Coachworks was established in Hanwell, in West London, and expanded its business to build similar sporting coachwork for a number of the less expensive makes. The Arrow specials were sold through Normand Garages in London's Oxford Street. Compton's company also built some special coachwork for the Seven under the Compton name *(qv)*.

Compton left the company in 1932 after financial problems arose, and Arrow was re-organised from late August that year. Although the company still focused on Austin Sevens, it now catered for a wider variety of makes and switched from Normand Garages to HA Saunders of Golders Green Road in north London. Later models were visually more derivative, and the company went out of business in 1935. Some of its last bodies were actually finished by Whittingham & Mitchel in Chelsea's Kings Road.

The Arrow Coupé of 1929 had metal panels that were covered in fabric to simulate the appearance of fashionable Weymann coachwork. The two doors were rear-hinged, and there was a shallow windscreen that was arranged to open forwards and carried a single wiper. The body had a low scuttle, no running-boards, and helmet-type front wings, while luggage was carried in the tail. The coupé cost £179 10s 0d.

It was followed in August 1929 by an open two-seater, which again took the Arrow

A 1932 Arrow Sports Foursome. (Matthew Barker)

This 1934 Arrow Sports Foursome was built on the 75in wheelbase chassis. (Robin Lawton)

brand name but was actually designed by GF Simmonds, the Secretary of the Cambridge University Automobile Club. Simmonds had built his own prototype with fabric panels, but when he offered the design to Compton Sons & Terry they chose to develop it further, changing to metal panels with a fabric covering as on their Coupé; the covering was a material called Fabrikloid.

The two-seater had a neat and shapely design, with a sloping tail. As was usual with hand-built designs, it evolved over time, and from early in 1930 the spare wheel was mounted externally on this tail. From July 1930 the original steel panels were changed for aluminium ones, and it appears that one body was built in February 1931 without the fabric covering – which by then had fallen out of fashion.

The next new design from Arrow was a four-seater called the Arrow Sports Foursome, and it appeared in June 1931. The body had conventionally painted aluminium panels on an ash frame, and its two doors had cutaway tops to give a semi-sporting appearance. There were no running-boards, and the spare wheel was again mounted externally on the tail, which in this case was quite upright. There was an arrow emblem on the grille, and the car came with a tonneau cover that doubled as a hood bag. These models remained in production after the Arrow company was re-organised, and of course evolved over time as well. In line with developments affecting the parent chassis, four-speed gearboxes replaced three-speed types during 1932. The earliest Sports Foursome models were on the 75in wheelbase, but later bodies were adapted to suit the 81in wheelbase and offered correspondingly more room. The long-wheelbase versions cost £155 in 1933, but it is not clear when the last ones were built or how many were made.

After lead designer Arthur Compton left, Arrow took a different tack, and their later bodies for the Austin Seven were very much inspired by the 1932 MG J-type. They had a slab tank mounted externally at the rear with the spare wheel mounted on it, and flowing, swept front wings that became running-boards before meeting the rear wings. These bodies were always mounted on the Sports version of the Seven chassis, initially the EB or AEB Nippy and later the EK or AEK Speedy.

The first ones were built in October 1933, and were known as the Arrow Competition 65, but the name later changed to Arrow Special 65 Sports. The price was £184 in February 1934, rising to £189 by 1935. The Arrow Special 75 Sports arrived in February 1935 and cost £207, and when Austin started supplying chassis with 17in wheels, these became standard on all models in place of the earlier 19in size. A supercharger option became available during 1935 for an extra £37, and when fitted to the AEK model this produced a car known as the Arrow Competition Two-seater. There is no evidence of production numbers for any of these cars.

A 1934 Arrow Competition 65. (Robin Lawton)

BOYD-CARPENTER

FH Boyd-Carpenter worked for Gordon England, and from 1926 raced Sevens at Brooklands. That year, he established Boyd-Carpenter Ltd at the old Gordon England service depot in Kilburn, London. He was soon joined by fellow Seven racer HN Thompson and the company became Boyd-Carpenter & Thompson Ltd, which specialised in tuning Austin Sevens.

In 1928, the BC Special Austin 7 was announced as a complete package at £197 10s 0d. The engine was effectively blueprinted, with a lightened and balanced crankshaft assembly, modified pistons, a reprofiled camshaft and enlarged and polished valve ports. For a further £25, an OHV conversion using the LAP cylinder head could be ordered, and either a special Claudel Hobson carburettor or twin carburettors were available. The chassis was modified with lowered springs that had extra leaves, while the steering column was steeply raked and a remote gear lever helped keep height down for the special bodywork.

This was of all-aluminium construction, with no doors, a long pointed tail, a fairing below the radiator grille, and cycle wings. The spare wheel was mounted alongside the scuttle on the passenger's side, and both bonnet and side valances were louvred. The seats were set as low as possible and featured pneumatic cushions. When tested by *Motor Sport* in September 1930, the car achieved a maximum speed of 71mph.

Sales were handled by the London dealer Normand Garage, and by 1931 the price had dropped to £192 10s 0d. Normand also sold the BC Austin Junior, a less expensive model introduced in January 1931 as a semi-sports type with proper doors and with the spare wheel mounted externally on a squared-up tail.

The best estimate is that 31 or 32 of these cars were built, but that figure includes similar "specials" on the Wolseley Hornet and also one on a Standard chassis. Very few of the Boyd-Carpenter Sevens survive.

The Boyd-Carpenter company was itself very active in motor racing, and successfully campaigned a pair of Austin Seven "specials" that were known as Mr and Mrs Jo-Jo. Mr Jo-Jo was a tuned Gordon England Cup model that was used for long-distance record attempts, and Mrs Jo-Jo was a circuit racer that Boyd-Carpenter had developed from one of the streamlined Gordon England Brooklands models (see Chapter 7).

This is a 1930 Boyd-Carpenter Special. The hat seems somewhat out of sympathy with the reclined driving position.

The Boyd-Carpenter Junior was a less radical and considerably cheaper design that was also available for the Morris Minor chassis. This is a December 1930 advertisement.

The three London branches of Normand Garage handled Boyd-Carpenter models.

The tail of this 1930 Boyd-Carpenter car appears to be rather longer than the one in contemporary pictures. (Clive Barker)

BRIGHTON

There was probably only ever one Sports Saloon Coupé body on a Seven chassis from the Brighton Grand Garage and Coachbuilding Works. It was built for the manager of this south coast company in 1926 and had aluminium panels on an ash frame.

The design combined a two-door coupé body with a boat-fail rear end, under which the spare wheel was carried. The bonnet was specially manufactured and louvred, and there was a luggage platform behind the two seats in the body.

BURGHLEY

1926 Burghley Sports in bare aluminium. (Clive Barker)

Wilson Motors of Victoria in London was one of the earliest independent coachbuilders to offer bodies for the Austin Seven. The company used the brand name of Burghley for the two designs it announced in 1924.

The Burghley Sports was a boat-tailed two-seater with both fashionable ship-type ventilators on its scuttle and walnut deck planking and copper nails as features of its rear body. Fashionable splayed wings were offered initially, but from February 1926 a raked style was available as an alternative, and the length of the tail was increased. The car was built on a production chassis with a steeply raked steering column, and early models were fitted with a phosphor-bronze cylinder head that was claimed to deliver 55mph and 50mpg.

ACE wheel discs and Triplex windscreen glass were available as extras, but the basic car cost £195 in 1924, reducing to £185 in 1925 and £175 in 1926. It was still being advertised in 1928, by which time the price was £182 or, with aluminium wings, £187. There is no information available about production numbers.

The second of those 1924 designs was a Saloon Landaulette, which qualifies it as the first attempt by a coachbuilder to make a Saloon-type body for the Seven. The body was once again panelled in aluminium, and it appears that the whole of the roof folded down, leaving the cantrails and side windows in place. This arrangement made it more of a folding-roof Saloon than a Landaulette, although that name certainly made it sound more grand. It was priced at £195 in 1927 and 1928 but once again, there is no information about production quantities.

The Burghley Sports had all the fashionable design cues incorporated in a single model.

Burghley's Saloon Landaulette of 1924 was first in a very small field.

CADOGAN

Cadogan Motors was based in London's Fulham district by the late 1920s, having been in Chelsea until 1927, when the company went through a financial reconstruction. Its reputation was for stylish coachwork, and that may explain why it was the choice of one Captain O'Hagan, the designer with Van den Plas coachworks of Brussels, when he wanted a special individual car on an Austin Seven chassis.

The chassis was lengthened by 18 inches to give a wheelbase of 93 inches, and the frame side members were lowered by 7 inches. The body, which O'Hagan designed in close collaboration with Cadogan, was a low-slung fabric-panelled coupé, with a long bonnet, dummy landau irons, wheel discs and cycle wings. Just the one car appears to have been built, in early 1929, although the coachbuilder did offer to construct replicas.

The Cadogan-bodied Seven was known as the OH Special after Captain O'Hagan who ordered it. The extra 18 inches of wheelbase made it almost unrecognisable as an Austin Seven.

COLE & SHUTTLEWORTH

The Cole & Shuttleworth partnership operated from premises in Fulham, south-west London, and may have had close ties with other London coachbuilders such as William Cole & Sons of Hammersmith. It is almost certain that the company's design for a Sports body on the Austin Seven was later continued by KC Bodies, who operated from the same address (see below).

The Sport body was introduced in 1926 and was mounted on an otherwise standard Seven chassis with a 4.4:1 axle ratio and a more steeply raked steering column to allow lower lines. The aluminium-panelled body had a boat-tail design, and in the top of that tail was a hatch that gave access to the luggage compartment and spare wheel stowage. A divided windscreen and cycle-type wings contributed to the necessary sporting aura.

The model cost £175 and was available until 1928. There is no known record of production quantities.

The Cole & Shuttleworth Sport had a fashionable boat-tail body. (Motorsport Images)

COMPTON

The intricate details of Arthur P Compton's many business ventures need not disrupt the story here; suffice it to say that AP Compton & Co built not only Arrow bodies *(qv)* at their premises in Hanwell but also bodies using their own name. Compton also seems to have minimised any clash of interests by ensuring that the bodies bearing his own name were distributed by HA Saunders in north London while the Arrow bodies went through Normand Garages in London's West End.

The first of these Compton bodies was announced in September 1930 and was known as the Spear. It was a pointed-tail two-seater mounted on a standard Seven chassis with raked steering column. Distinctive features included a polished aluminium rear deck and a sporty cutaway at the top of the driver's door, while the passenger had a simple straight door top.

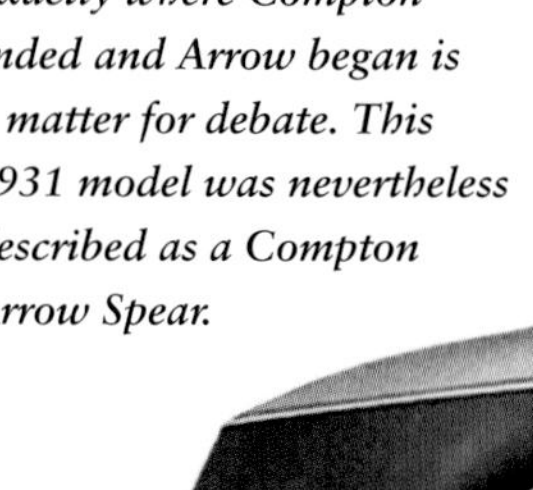

Exactly where Compton ended and Arrow began is a matter for debate. This 1931 model was nevertheless described as a Compton Arrow Spear.

The body was of course ash-framed and had cellulosed metal panels, with cycle-type wings and with the spare wheel carried at the side, just ahead of the driver's door. The bonnet panel was longer than any seen on any of the Arrow products up to that time, which helped the car look a little longer and sleeker, and a vertical strip on the grille was a further distinguishing feature. The folding hood was made of duck and the car cost £160.

Adding a little more confusion to the various Compton bodies, the Arrow Lance Coupé was introduced just a few months after the Spear in February 1931. Was it an Arrow, or a Compton Arrow? Or were the advertising arrangements simply inconsistent? One way or another, this £155 coupé carried its spare wheel on the tail panel and had steel panels on an ash frame. It also reverted to the earlier Arrow practice of covering the external surfaces with Fabrikloid. That fashion throwback seems not to have been a major hindrance to sales because the model was still being offered for sale three years later in 1934, when it was listed at £184. However, there is no way of knowing how many (if any) had been built in the intervening three years.

COX

The Cox Sports Tourer is known only from a surviving example that dates from late 1927, and nothing is known about the coachbuilder. Bryan Purves suggested that the company might have been based in London, although the car's registration number was issued in Berkshire.

This Sports Tourer had an ash frame, a wooden floor panel, and aluminium panelling with a fashionable fabric covering. The body design was very simple, with a pointed tail, cycle wings and a folding fabric hood.

CWS

The story of the CWS saloon is a mildly amusing one, if nothing else. When the CWS furniture factory was destined for closure, the workshop manager suggested a move into car bodywork. His own Gordon England Fabric Saloon served as the prototype, and his reworked version impressed the CWS Directors enough for them to agree to the purchase of five chassis from Austin. One of these became involved in a misadventure that twisted the chassis, leading to the collapse of the body and the end of the CWS bodybuilding enterprise. The date is believed to have been 1928.

DUPLE

Duple Bodies & Motors Ltd was established in the London Borough of Hornsey in 1919, and after a move to Hendon in 1926 became one of Britain's leading makers of coach bodies. Founder Herbert White had briefly built cars under the Bifort name at Fareham in Hampshire during 1914. The Bifort had been a car that could be transformed into a van, and the Duple name was intended to suggest the same versatility. Duple's first activities were fitting bodies of this type to ex-military Ford Model Ts, and it was not long before the company tried the same thing for the Austin Seven.

The Duple Convertible was announced in July 1926, just after the move to Hendon. It was based on the recently-announced Type R saloon, which Duple modified behind the doors so that either a van body or a touring body could be fitted. The touring body came with a folding hood, detachable side screens, and a detachable rear seat. The van body, which had aluminium panels on an ash frame and twin rear doors, bolted to the same mounting points. Duple asked £180 for the model, complete with its two interchangeable back bodies, and reduced that to £177 during 1927. No production figures are known, but the Convertible was not a notable success.

Duple tried again in July 1927, this time with a conventional Two-seater body made of aluminium panels on an ash frame. This was a semi-sports type, with a folding hood and a pointed tail that was provided with a hatch for access to the compartment within; the spare wheel was slung underneath. The wings and running-boards were of Austin provenance, and every Duple Two-seater came in two colours, the darker one being applied to the wings and the upper body panels. The car initially cost £165, plus the delivery charge of the chassis from Austin.

The Duple Convertible evolved along with the Seven itself, and its headlights moved from the scuttle to the wings in autumn 1927. From September 1927, Duple modified the hatch in the tail so that a dickey seat could be fitted, and modified the hood as well so that the two would not interfere with one another. At the same time, the price was dropped to £155. Duple hedged their bets by offering the body alone for DIY fitting at a cost of just £53 10s 0d, and from the start of production they added a charge of £3 for leather upholstery.

Duple Bodies and Motors, Ltd., of Hendon, London, N.W., is marketing a convertible body for the Austin Seven chassis which enables this handy little vehicle to be used for business or pleasure purposes. These pictures show how speedy and simple it is to effect the conversion.

The first Duple-bodied Seven was the Convertible, which could be turned from Tourer to Van by swapping body sections. The van body here has square-cut cab window openings, unlike the contemporary Startin type.

The Duple Two-seater of 1927 was an altogether more conventional body. (Clive Barker)

GODFREY & PROCTOR

There may well have been only one Godfrey & Proctor Sports car, which essentially combined Austin Seven components with a special long-wheelbase chassis frame and an open two-seater body made of aluminium. The car was built by Ron Godfrey (of GN and, later, HRG fame) and Stuart Proctor and was raced at Brooklands in 1928. Its special 93-inch wheelbase chassis was designed by Godfrey specifically to take Austin Seven components and was built by GN.

GRUZELLIER

Absolutely nothing is known about Alan Gruzellier & Co except that they were British and built at least one Sports body for an Austin Seven that was offered for sale in the May 1925 issue of *The Light Car and Cyclecar*. Its chassis appears to date from 1924 and its price of £185 was about par for such models at the time.

It is not clear how many Gruzellier bodies were built. This convincing replica surfaced in time for the Seven's 100th Anniversary. (Clive Barker)

HARTWELL

There was just one Hartwell Special, which was commissioned in 1929 by the Oxford car dealer George Hartwell for his son. The car was on a standard chassis with raked steering that allowed the driver to sit well back, while the springs were flattened and cord-bound and the front axle was a drop-centre type. The two-seater body was built by Hartwell's themselves from sheet aluminium and featured a short wasp tail and steeply upswept scuttle that obviated the need for an aero screen.

The Hartwell Special.

HAWK (MATCHLESS)

The Matchless motorcycle company decided to join the myriad companies offering special bodies for the Austin Seven by repurposing a section of its sidecar factory in Plumstead, south-east London. A two-seater body called the Hawk Sports was announced in September 1930, on a standard Seven chassis with raked steering column. (Matchless also introduced their Silver Hawk motorcycle that year.)

The Hawk had fabric panels on an ash frame, a suitably pointed tail and a radiator grille with a vertical central spine. This was a cycle-winged design, and the crossbar linking the front wings turned with them, so allowing the headlights to shine around corners. The model cost £150 and production continued into 1931, but there is no record of how many were made.

The two-seater Hawk Sports was bodied by motorcycle manufacturer, Matchless. (Motorsport Images)

HOYAL

The Hoyal Body Corporation was formed from the ashes of coachbuilder Hoyal & Chalmer in early 1926, taking its name from those of its partners, H Hamilton Hoyer and Henry Allingham. Expansion plans preceded by a re-formation in 1928 were abandoned, and the company turned its Weybridge works over to building bodies for buses and for a number of smaller and inexpensive chassis, which included the Austin Seven.

Hoyal had two designs for the Seven, one an open Two-seater and the other a Sports Saloon with two seats. Both appeared in 1928 and were probably still catalogued when Hoyal closed its doors in August 1931. Both were fabric-panelled bodies and the open one was also available for other chassis, such as the Morris Minor and Wolseley Hornet.

The open Two-seater was distinguished by its large boot, which nevertheless curved gracefully down at the tail and had the spare wheel mounted on its exterior. The car had louvred valances below its doors and was

Hoyal's open Two-seater of 1928 combined the practicality of a large boot with sporting cues such as the louvred panel alongside the chassis frame

initially offered with cycle wings, although later examples had full wings and running-boards. A distinguishing feature, which was also applied to the Sports Saloon, was a flash in contrasting colour just below each door window. The Two-seater was priced at £150, but the body could be ordered on its own for mounting by the purchaser, when it cost £55 10s 0d. By 1930, the price for the complete car had risen to £170, which was perhaps indicative of the difficulties Hoyal were in at a time when other prices tended to be falling. The Sports Saloon cost £172 in standard form or £182 with a de luxe finish.

HUGHES

Thomas Hughes & Son were makers of motorcycle sidecars in the Sparkhill district of Birmingham, and in 1924 turned their hand to a sporting body for the Austin Seven. The Hughes Sports had aluminium panels over an ash frame, no doors, and a vee windscreen, and the spare wheel was carried below the pointed tail that followed the style of the Alvis 12/50 "duck's back" model. There were two ship-type ventilators on the scuttle panel, but there were no side screens for the neat hood. The model was built on a standard Austin Seven chassis, its appearance somewhat marred by an exhaust slung below the rear axle rather than mounted less vulnerably higher up. No details are available of price or production numbers.

JARROT

Jarrot Motor Bodies had their works at Wednesbury in the West Midlands and were probably established in 1919. According to a letter in *Motor Sport* for February 1969, the company mainly specialised in body repairs but occasionally built bodies for Model T Fords. Jarrot was not very sound financially in its early days, but in 1926 its proprietor took on a partner.

After that, the company started making bodies for the Austin Seven and its fortunes improved. Bryan Purves dates the start of production to 1928 and notes that the engines were tuned by skimming the cylinder head to increase the compression ratio. The *Motor Sport* letter notes that the bodies were most attractive and similar to a Bugatti Type 35. Supposedly about 35 had been built (some on new chassis and others on old chassis supplied by customers) before Jarrot Motor Bodies collapsed in 1931.

JARVIS

Jarvis & Sons Ltd, of Wimbledon, proudly advertised itself as the designer and builder of this Coupette body in 1927.

Jarvis & Son Ltd was a coachbuilder in Wimbledon, south-west London, which earned itself a reputation during the 1920s for sports and racing bodies. That it should create a folding-head two-seater on the Austin Seven chassis is therefore no great surprise. This made its appearance in September 1927.

Jarvis chose to call its body a Coupette; ARC Manufacturing (see above) used the same description for an Austin Seven body in the same year. It was a two-seater with a very distinctive detachable hood design that featured a diamond-shaped rear window and an unusually flat roof. Jarvis charged £177 when the design was new, but it is impossible to say how many examples were eventually built.

JENSEN

When the brothers Richard and Alan Jensen built their first car on the basis of a 1923 Austin Seven in 1928, it was the start of a long journey that would eventually turn them into the owners of a well-respected sports car company. They turned it into a low-slung two-seater Sports with all the fashionable styling cues of the time – cycle wings, a boat-tail, and louvred bonnet side panels – and added a redesigned radiator shell based on that of a Sunbeam.

A later rebuild saw them replace the cycle wings with a long, flowing style that incorporated running-boards. The car was spotted by someone who worked at Standard, and the Jensen brothers were invited to design a car for them. That eventually became the Avon-Standard two-seater.

There was only ever one Austin Seven-based "Jensen Special no 1".

The one and only Jensen Special had a considerable amount of style, and started a successful career for its creators.

KC

KC Bodies operated from the same address in London's Fulham district as Cole & Shuttleworth (see above), and was very probably a further evolution of the same company. Its first bodies appear to have been made in 1928, the year when Cole & Shuttleworth ceased their business.

The first offering on the Austin Seven from KC Bodies was announced in May 1928 and was a two-seater cycle-winged Sports model that has some similarities with the body built by Cole & Shuttleworth between 1926 and 1928. The main difference is that the KC version had steel rather than aluminium panels (presumably for cost reasons). KC charged £175 for their car – the same as the Cole & Shuttleworth Sports – and by 1930 that price had increased to £185.

This initial model became known as the Standard type when it was supplemented later in the year by Special Sports and Super Sports models. The Special Sports had the same body design but (according to Bryan Purves) was tuned by KC with modified pistons, larger valves and a free-flow exhaust system. In this guise, its estimated top speed was 65mph. The Super Sports also used the original body design but its engine was supercharged and KC estimated its top speed at between 70mph and 75mph.

The KC range was re-introduced during 1929 as a three-model range that now included

The KC Bodies design may well have evolved from the earlier one by Cole & Shuttleworth.

a model with underslung chassis that was named the Ulster – apparently before Austin's own Ulster model reached the public. The range began with the KC Special at £168 10s 0d that had a standard production engine. Above that came the KC Special Sports with a tuned engine and a price of £182, and at the top of the range the Ulster type cost £204; this probably had the supercharged engine from the earlier KC Super Sports model.

As is so often the case with the products of independent coachbuilders, there are no surviving records to indicate how many of these cars were built. KC Bodies was still active in 1931, but it is likely that there were no more bodies for the Seven after 1930.

MADDOX

During the 1920s, George Maddox & Sons was a successful and versatile coachbuilder in Huntingdon, Cambridgeshire. Towards the end of the decade it began to focus on less expensive chassis, and among these was the Austin Seven.

The company's only known design on the Seven was called the Arrow Coupé, which cost £185 and was a drophead two-seater model. Bryan Purves dates this to 1930 but Nick Walker (*A-Z British Coachbuilders*) suggests 1931, the year in which the company converted to limited company status. There is no indication how many Arrow Coupés might have been built.

MARTIN WALTER

Martin Walter Ltd began coachbuilding in 1914 after buying out a local coachbuilder to supplement its motor vehicle repairs business.

It is perhaps a shame that there was only ever one Romney Coupé by Martin Walter, which was a most attractive and well-resolved design.

This in turn had grown out of a business established in around 1773 as a saddle-maker, which had moved to Folkestone approximately a century later. The company built on a variety of chassis in the interwar years, although most were far more grand than the Austin Seven.

The company's only known body for the Austin Seven was a special order for the daughter of one of its Directors. It was a neat folding-head two-seater that was built on a production type AE Tourer chassis and featured a neatly curved boot with a large hinged lid. The car seems to have been completed in June 1930 and was known as the Romney Coupé.

MAYTHORN

The Maythorn Coupé was another attractive one-off.

The Maythorn coachworks was established at Biggleswade in Bedfordshire in 1842, and the son of the founder expanded into car body building at the start of the 20th century. By then known as Maythorn & Son Ltd, the company became a subsidiary of the coachbuilder Hooper in 1920, although the two companies retained their individual identities.

Maythorn bodies were normally confined to grand chassis such as Daimler, Rolls-

Royce and Bentley, but in 1927 an American customer persuaded the company to build a neat three-box Coupé on an Austin Seven chassis. The car was supposedly used at the family's home in West Palm Beach, Florida, and remained unique.

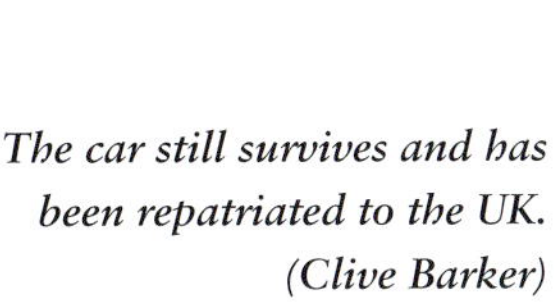

The car still survives and has been repatriated to the UK. (Clive Barker)

MERLYN

Merlyn Motors Ltd of Bristol were primarily car dealers but they also dabbled in other fields, such as outboard motors for boats. In June 1929, they built the body for the Merlyn Coupé, designed by architect RA Duncan.

The body had a fixed roof over the passenger compartment and a folding rear roof. Beading on the body side and an absence of running-boards were intended to accentuate the overall length of the car, although the success of that idea was certainly questionable. The price was quoted as £185 but it is doubtful whether more than one example was ever built.

The Merlyn Coupé was a very neat design and versatile, too, with a folding rear roof section. (Motorsport Images)

NEW AVON

The Avon coachworks was founded in Warwick in 1919, and was re-organised three years later as the New Avon Body Co Ltd. For most of the 1920s its main work came from Lea-Francis, but from 1927 New Avon began to branch out. That year, the company announced its first special body for the Austin Seven. New Avon is believed to have bought 30 chassis from Austin, of which three were sold on to Swallow. Of the remaining 27, 26 were supposedly bodied as Tourers and just one as a Semi-sports (although this may not be the whole story because, as the following makes clear, New Avon offered other body styles for the Seven as well).

The first body was a semi-sports Two-seater that was introduced in July 1927. It had a tapered boat tail that contained a large locker for luggage and tools, to which access was gained through a hatch on the top; the spare wheel was hung on the reverse-rake tail panel. Although the chassis was essentially standard, New Avon added their own wings to give the finished vehicle a more sporting air and, of course, did not fit running-boards. This was a quality production, with a double-duck folding hood, celluloid side curtains, and antique leather upholstery. As the body was a straightforward

This 1929 example of the Avon sports body with toned-down tail end shows what a delightful little car it was. (Clive Barker)

fit on the standard Seven chassis, Avon offered it for fitting at home for just £52, or of course would supply a complete car for £164.

The second body was announced a year later, and was actually designed by the Jensen brothers who had already created a special body for New Avon on a Standard chassis. (The brothers' first car had been an Austin Seven, a 1923 saloon bought second-hand that they immediately stripped down and turned into the very attractive Jensen Special No 1.)

BEFORE you order that AUSTIN SEVEN

SEE the AVON "SWAN"

COUPE £159

Special Cup Winner at Concours d'Elegance, Southport.

With opening sunshine roof — generous equipment — 3 colour choice, Red, Blue, Black.

AND the AVON "SPORTSMAN"

TWO-SEATER £148

A Fabric Duo-Colour Body.
Two large doors.
Sloping single panel opening screen.
Pneumatic cushions.
Scuttle ventilators.
Ample luggage room.
Very roomy, 40 in. between doors.

Manufactured by— THE NEW AVON BODY CO., Ltd., WARWICK.

Main Agents:
The Car Mart Ltd., 46/50, Park Lane, W., and 297, Euston Rd., N.W.1 LONDON AND ESSEX.
Frank Hallam, 18-20, Bristol St., B'ham. BIRMINGHAM DISTRICT.
Lookers, Ltd., Deansgate, Manchester. LANCASHIRE AND CHESHIRE.
Martin Walter Ltd. - - Folkestone. KENT.

The special-bodied Sevens from New Avon were available over quite a large geographical area.

This second New Avon Seven special was called the Swan Coupé, and was a striking-looking two-seater machine with a deliberately tall body that had a roll-back sunshine roof. The body had an ash frame and plywood panels that were covered in fashionable fabric; the bonnet sides were louvred (long before Austin did this as standard) and there was a small boot at the rear with the spare wheel mounted vertically on its outside. The seats were trimmed in moquette, and the wheels were painted white with all exterior coachwork colours. The Swan Coupé cost £156.

The Swan Coupé was made available on Standard chassis as well, and the coachbuilder's success with this and other bodies for Standard kept the workforce busy until 1937. In the mean time, there was just one more special body for the Austin Seven, this time the Sportsman's Two-seater announced in July 1929. Mounted on the contemporary Sports chassis with raked steering column, this was another open semi-sports body which could be had with either fabric or painted metal panels – a wise precaution as a backlash against the poor durability of fabric panels was already beginning. It had luggage accommodation within a tapered tail, and access to this was through a hatch on the rear deck.

The Sportsman's Two-seater had a louvred bonnet that was 3in longer than the one on the Swan Coupé to make the car appear longer. It had small scuttle ventilators (again, long before Austin introduced them), cycle wings and, of course, no running-boards. The folding hood was again made of duck and there were celluloid side curtains and antique leather upholstery again. The model was introduced at £148 but by late 1929 its price had increased to £159.

Avon's Sportsman's Two Seater was announced in July 1929. (Clive Barker)

PYTCHLEY

Pytchley Autocar was an established car dealer and coachbuilder in Northampton by 1925, when it announced its new sliding roof design (which would later often be called a sunshine roof). Within a few years, sliding roofs were commonplace on British cars, and most were provided by Pytchley themselves. Austin bought Pytchley sunroofs for its Seven models.

Despite the huge success of its new product, Pytchley did not renounce its coachbuilding business and in 1928 introduced a complete Saloon body for the Austin Seven, apparently with fabric skin panels. This featured the company's patented sliding roof, cycle-type wings and no running-boards. It is not clear how many were made.

No Pytchley-bodied Austin Sevens survive but Malcolm Parker built a replica from a photo. It lacks the sunroof of the original car.

SALMONS

Coachbuilder Salmons & Sons was located at Newport Pagnell in Buckinghamshire, and in 1925 developed and patented a roll-back roof conversion for Saloon cars. This was branded as the Tickford folding roof and was adaptable to cars of all sizes. It first became available for the Austin Seven in August 1929 and remained so well into the 1930s.

The Tickford Sunshine Saloon was strictly a conversion of an existing Saloon, and could be

The Salmons Tickford winding-head body is shown mid-way through its cycle here, with the detachable winding handle in place at the rear.

done on a brand-new car or on an older one. Salmons & Sons removed the roof and rear window and fitted a roll-back fabric roof that could be wound down by means of a removable handle inserted into a socket behind and below the left-hand rear side window.

In October 1931, Salmons charged £137 10s 0d for a brand-new Austin Seven with the Tickford sunshine roof; a De Luxe model with leather upholstery cost an extra £10. Conversions to existing Saloons could be done for £19 10s 0d.

There is no indication of how many Austin Seven Tickford Sunshine Saloons were made.

A surviving Tickford car is seen here with the roof in place. (Clive Barker)

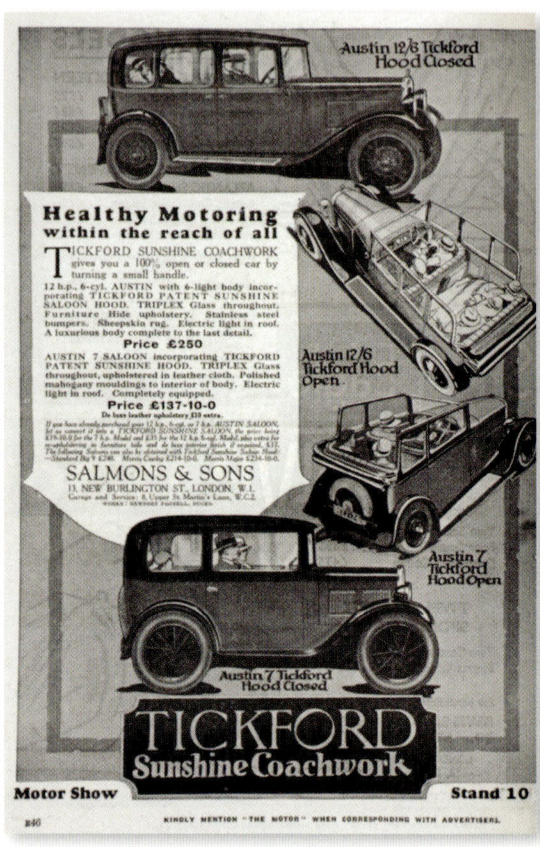

This 1931 advertisement for Tickford Sunshine Coachwork shows examples on the Austin Twelve as well as the Austin Seven.

STARTIN

As the contract with Austin to build Delivery Vans approached its end during 1930, Startin clearly determined to continue with what must have been a profitable line of business for as long as they could, and developed their own van body for fitting to the Seven chassis. These were of course sold alongside the new vans that Austin had started to build at Longbridge, but they remained in production only until the middle of 1931; perhaps potential customers considered that the Austin-built product was superior and demand for the Startin type tailed off.

These vans were initially built on the chassis of the Type AE Tourer that was their contemporary and had that model's short bonnet. When the AE Tourer was replaced by the AF model in June 1930, Startin of course built their van on this newer type of chassis. The van body was quite different from what had gone before. It had a fully enclosed cab with full-height doors that incorporated sliding windows, and a flat roof with a slight taper over the cab. Some pictures suggest that the spare wheel may have been carried on the roof, at least as an option to create more room within the body.

As usual, there is no reliable information about quantities. However, these vans were almost certainly built in smaller numbers than their Austin-made counterparts, and the relatively short production run must have ensured their rarity.

Startin's own-design van was only available for a short time after the company ceased building under contract to Austin.

T&D

T&D Motors was based in north-west London, and the company's only known foray into coachbuilding was a Sports Coupé for the Austin Seven that was announced in January 1931. Pictures show a car that was tall and narrow in appearance, with a fabric-covered roof that incorporated a sliding sunshine section. The whole was completed by cycle wings and a rear luggage compartment. Whether more than one example was ever built is not known.

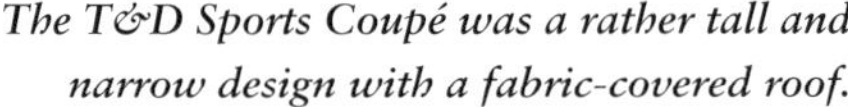

The T&D Sports Coupé was a rather tall and narrow design with a fabric-covered roof.

TAYLOR (LONDON)

H Taylor & Co was a London coachbuilder with premises in both Kensington and outside the city at Kingston in Surrey. Between 1927 and 1930 it built a number of special bodies for the Austin Seven, but its only other known work was for a Singer chassis in 1930.

Taylor's first Austin Seven design was a Semi-Sports type that was introduced in 1927. It had aluminium panels on an ash frame, and rode on a standard chassis with a more steeply raked steering column and minor modifications to suit the body mountings. The body had a rather pert appearance, with a high boot line that curved sharply downwards, and always came with a two-tone paint finish. The folding hood was accompanied by side screens, and a fixed backrest was accompanied by pneumatic cushions on the floor to give a low seating position.

The design developed over time. Early cars had only one door, on the passenger side, but later models had one on each side. The windscreen was initially flat, but was later changed to a vee-type. The original price of

£175 had been lowered to £158 by late 1928.

A second version of the design appeared during 1928, this time with slightly lower and more attractive lines that were matched by fabric panelling and a painted bonnet. A redesign at the rear allowed a single dickey seat to be fitted; the spare wheel was now carried on the tail and the folding hood sat more neatly on the body when lowered. The model was known as a Fabric Semi-sports, again came with a two-tone finish, and cost £160 or £170 when equipped with the optional dickey seat.

From June 1930, the Ace Semi-Sports appeared with detail improvements over the earlier Semi-Sports body. This time, the spare wheel was kept inside the tail in a lockable compartment, and there was a disappearing hood whose frame could also be stowed in the tail. This version of the design had semi-cycle wings and no running-boards, and also

Two-colour paintwork and a neat tail treatment characterised the Special Sports model from Taylor of London in 1927.

A surviving Taylor Semi Sports. (Clive Barker)

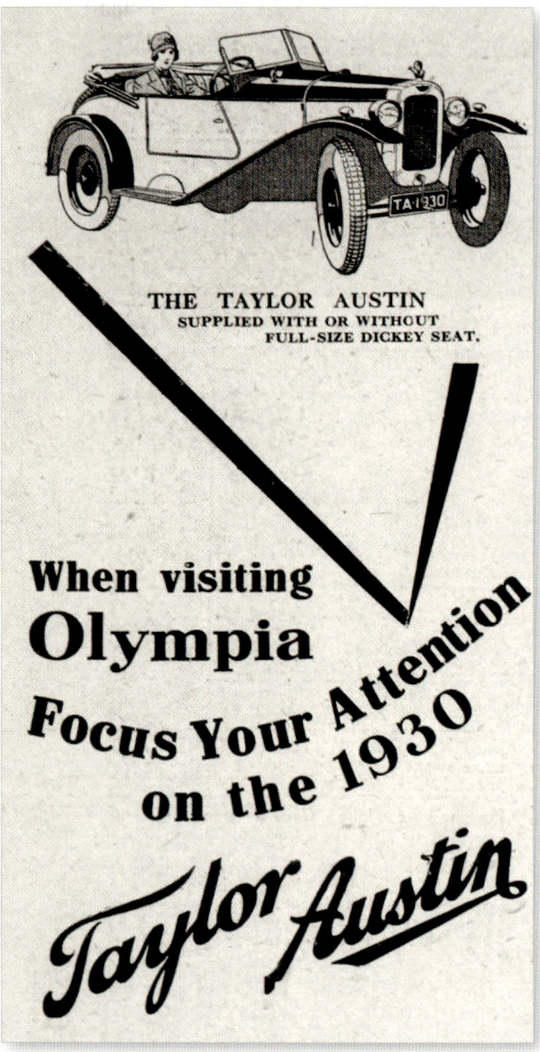

This advertisement from 1929 shows that a dickey seat option was available for the company's Special Sports model.

came with a strange (but removable) rear stabilising fin.

Meanwhile, a more deliberately sporting design called the Super Sports had appeared during 1928 alongside the Semi-Sports of the time. This had an aluminium body that was distinguished by raked front wings and by a long tail that overhung the rear by some distance and may have led to the model's alternative name of the Taylor Launch. The tail provided a good-sized locker and the spare wheel was mounted to it, while there was room below for a second spare to be carried. For good measure, there was an alternative fabric version of the body. Later examples had the spare wheel relocated within the tail, and were also supplied with fashionable polished wheel discs.

TAYLOR (WOLVERHAMPTON)

A second coachbuilder called Taylor introduced a Semi-sports body for the Austin Seven in 1927. This was Taylor Bodies of Wolverhampton, who became better known after 1929 as Holbrook & Taylor. There is very little information available about these models, and no production figures are known.

WATERMAN

Very little is known about Waterman Coaches of Spaxton in Somerset, although surviving Austin records do confirm that they were supplied with six examples of the Seven chassis during 1929.

Just one Waterman-bodied car is known to survive, and that is an aluminium-panelled Tourer whose design seems to have been adapted from the contemporary AD Tourer. It was put on the road in August 1929 and was registered locally in Somerset.

WYLDER

G Wylder & Co were coachbuilders based just outside London at Kew in Surrey, and during the late 1920s built a number of fabric bodies for various Austin chassis. Wide doors were a common design element, and these bodies were known as Wydoor types. The version for the Seven chassis was announced in September 1927 and was a Saloon with blind rear quarters that carried dummy landau irons. A set of Austin-supplied wings and running-boards was used, and the bodies had an unusual D-shaped rear window, with the spare wheel mounted below it on the tail panel.

Wylder's Wydoor model was a Saloon that was made to look like a more raffish Coupé. (Motorsport Images)

WORKS SPEED AND COMPETITION CARS

Central to the story of the works racing Austin Sevens is Arthur Waite, who was Herbert Austin's son-in-law and a Director of the Austin Company. Waite was an Australian, who had met Austin's daughter Irene while in hospital with injuries sustained at Gallipoli. The two were married in 1918.

After the end of the First World War, Captain Waite joined the Austin company, and in 1920 he was able to persuade Sir Herbert that racing would bring in valuable publicity for the Austin marque in general. He then embarked on a programme of designing and building competition models, and turned his attention to the Seven when it became available in 1922. By spring 1923 he had prepared a racing Seven which he campaigned with considerable success at the Brooklands track and also at the Monza track in Italy.

In 1925, a formal Racing Department was established at the Longbridge factory, and Waite's first programme for the Seven was to create a supercharged car. The one that he and his team developed won the 500 Mile Handicap event at Brooklands with Waite himself at the wheel during 1925. He continued to campaign specially-prepared Sevens, and by the end of 1928 he personally held all the Class H (750cc) speed records.

During 1927, Waite returned to Australia to help establish the Austin distributorship in Melbourne. While there, he asked for his supercharged single-seater to be shipped out to Australia so that he could compete in the 100 Miles Road Race to be held on Phillip Island in March 1928. However, by this stage his car had been stripped of its engine and sold on, so Austin sent a supercharged Sports model instead, and with this Waite went on to win the under-2000cc class at the Phillip Island event, which later became known as the first Australian Grand Prix.

From 1930, Waite was back in England, and works racing at Austin took on a new lease of life. A new team of works racers derived from the successful Super Sports achieved success in

When Austin provided Arthur Waite with a substitute car for a 1928 event in Australia, he still managed to win it.

that year's Brooklands 500 Mile Handicap, and for the next few years Austin took its racing very seriously, establishing permanent workshops at both the Brooklands and Donington circuits to oversee testing of the works racers. By 1934, however, it was clear that the Seven was no longer competitive in road and track events, and so Waite refocused the works competition efforts onto reliability trials.

Lord Austin accepted that it would no longer be possible to race cars based on the production Seven, and approved the development of a new model to compete in the 750cc class that Austin had made its own. The so-called Twin Cam racer that appeared in 1935 very quickly became the fastest car in its class, but of course it was not related to a production model and it was the last works racer from Austin.

GORDON ENGLAND SINGLE-SEATER, 1923

This car was not produced by the Austin works, but it had a profound influence on the development of competition Sevens at Austin – and, of course, Austin give its corporate blessing to several models later produced under the Gordon England name.

Gordon England, about whom there is more in Chapter 7, was convinced early on that the Austin Seven had competition potential, and in early 1923 built his own single-seat racer with a fully streamlined body. The car tasted success at Brooklands, but what made Austin sit up and take notice was when it out-performed Arthur Waite in the works car at the Whitsun meeting. Later modified in line with the works' "Boulogne" racers (see below), the car was turned into a two-seater later in 1923, and served as the prototype for the Gordon England Brooklands models.

In 1925, England decided to improve the aerodynamics of his racer, and redeveloped it with a heavily cowled radiator and a lower driving position that allowed a more streamlined long-tail body. He also raised the axle ratio to 4.1:1 to allow a higher top speed. At least one more similar car was built.

One of these two cars was then rebodied by FH Boyd-Carpenter, who worked for Gordon England and gave the car the name of Mrs Jo-Jo. Later still, the car was rebodied by Spero and, with the same name, went on to win the 750cc class in the 1928 JCC 200 mile race.

The Gordon England single-seater was known as the "Barrel" car, and in this photograph taken in 1923 it is not hard to see why.

"BOULOGNE" CARS, 1923

Arthur Waite at the wheel of "Dingo" , one of the Boulogne racers at Grand Prix des Voiturettes des Boulogne, September 1923. His riding mechanic was Alf Depper. (A7CA Archive)

The factory was developing a team of three racers, however, these weren't going to be ready for the early 1923 races, so the first proper "works" racer was the one created by Arthur Waite in early 1923. It was a fabric-bodied two-seater with no doors, and was based on a standard production chassis. It won its first race at Brooklands, the Easter Small Car Handicap held on 23 March 1923. Satisfied that it was reliable, Waite next took it to Italy for the 250km Cycle-car Grand Prix at Monza on 4 May. Here, he won the 750cc class, achieving a fastest lap of 64mph and gaining the distinction of achieving the first victory by a British car on the continent since the war.

The three "works" team cars were entered in the BARC Summer and August events, and by August were capable of lapping Brooklands at 75mph. The engines – developed from the standard 747cc four-cylinder which had 10.5bhp – were by then producing 29bhp at 4700rpm and could rev to 5000rpm. They had twin updraught Cox-Atmos carburettors, special cylinder heads, camshafts and valve springs, a 6.8:1 compression ratio, cast aluminium crankcases, and pressure lubrication that was achieved by drilling the crankshaft. They also had 4.5:1 axle gearing.

Keen to repeat the continental success at Monza, Austin entered all three cars for the Boulogne Motor Week that was held during

Lou King drove "Opossum" with his riding mechanic, Len Brockas. (A7CA Archive)

"Boomer" was driven by Harold Cutler along with his riding mechanic, R. E. O. Hall. (A7CA Archive)

September 1923, but this time without success. Two of the cars retired with lubrication failure and the third crashed.

The Boulogne cars were raced throughout 1924, and at Le Mans that year Arthur Waite came third and Austin team driver Roddis came fourth in the 750 cc class for the Grand Prix des Voiturettes. However, by the end of the year it was clear that the cars were no longer competitive and they were therefore retired.

SUPERCHARGED RACER, 1925

The next step in Arthur Waite's racing programme was to achieve a greater power output from the Seven's side-valve engine. The lubrication problems of the Boulogne cars had been identified and countered, and Waite decided to find the extra power he wanted by using a Roots-type supercharger. This helped to produce 36bhp at 5000rpm – a figure that with further development would be increased to very nearly 40bhp.

The supercharged engine was put into a specially constructed single-seat racer. The Austin Seven chassis was extended by 12in to allow the driver to sit as low as possible, and the engine was fitted slightly further back than standard to make room for the supercharger. A very low-slung body was created, with fabric panels over an ash frame.

In April 1925, Waite used this car to set a flying start mile speed of 94.02mph. With George Duller at the wheel, it won the 1925 Brooklands 500 mile Handicap at an average speed of 89.9mph – and broke its crankshaft just as it passed the finishing post.

With the engine and gearbox removed, it was then sold to an Austin employee, John Pares. With the assistance of others, he gave it an unsupercharged engine similar to the Gordon England Brooklands type, and the car had a further career under the name of Slippery Anne, setting some records at Brooklands and achieving some class successes at Shelsley Walsh. The original car was written off after an accident on the road, but a Slippery Anne recreation was built in 2021.

WORKS TT CARS, 1930

The success of the production Super Sports model, whose use of a supercharger had been presaged by Arthur Waite's 1925 Supercharged Racer, persuaded Austin management to go ahead with a new team of racers for the 1930 season.

At least five cars (and possibly six) were built; four were supercharged and one was not. Their high-revving engines delivered a claimed 46bhp at 6000rpm and drove through a close-ratio three-speed gearbox. The aluminium bodywork was similar to that of the Super Sports but had a deeper pointed tail that accommodated the spare wheel vertically. There were cycle-type wings and a steel bonnet.

The cars competed in several events at Brooklands and also in Ulster (when structural failure of the cylinder block caused a problem). Austin made much of their success in the 1930 Brooklands 500 Mile Handicap, when Sammy Davis and Freddy March won the event with an average speed of 83.41mph.

Sammy Davis and Freddie March won the 500-mile race at Brooklands in 1930 at an average speed of 83.41mph with this "works" TT car.

THE CAMPBELL SINGLE-SEATER, 1931

Austin prepared a special supercharged single-seater for record attempts and presented it to Sir Malcolm Campbell. It was based on a modified Type EA Sports chassis with an engine that produced 56bhp at 6000rpm and drove through a prototype four-speed gearbox (as Chapter 4 shows, four-speed gearboxes would not reach production until autumn 1932). The body was fabric-covered on an ash frame, with an aluminium fairing on each side to cover the chassis and running gear, and was painted in Campbell's favoured blue.

Campbell took the car with him to the USA when he went to Daytona Beach with the Bluebird Land Speed Record car. After taking the record at 246mph on 5 February 1931 in Bluebird, he made several attempts to set new records with the Seven, eventually raising the measured international Class H record to 94.03mph.

The car remained in the USA and for a time was displayed in the offices of the American Austin Company.

Campbell achieved records with this single-seater provided by Austin after taking the World Land Speed Record in his Bluebird car.

SALOON TRIALS CAR, 1931

Sir Herbert Austin was always most insistent that competition and record-breaking cars based on the Seven should resemble the showroom models as closely as possible. Possibly the closest the Racing Department got to this ideal was a Saloon model that was prepared for trials events in 1931.

The host car was a 1930 Fabric Saloon, which looked standard but had been prepared by the Racing Department with an Ulster TT engine, a prototype four-speed close-ratio gearbox, and stronger springs as fitted to the Seven vans that were cord-bound and gaitered. Three different axle ratios were used, and a choice was made to suit the event in hand.

This car was campaigned in trials events during 1931 and 1932 by Wallis Milton and Freddie Henry.

STREAMLINED RACER, 1931

By the winter of 1930-1931, Austin's domination of the 750cc class was subject to increasingly serious challenge, not least from MG. Just 11 days after Sir Malcolm Campbell had claimed the international Class H record at Daytona, George Eyston took an MG to Montlhéry and not only broke the record but also exceeded 100mph.

This must have been what prompted Arthur Waite to set the Austin Racing Department the task of producing their own 100mph car – based, of course, on a Seven. An off-set

Austin's supercharged, streamlined record car at Brooklands. Leon Cushman is at the wheel, having driven it to a two-way kilometre record of over 102mph, taking the 750cc class record from George Eyston and MG.

propellor shaft allowed the driver to sit low down, and the streamlined body showed the clear influence of Campbell's Bluebird Land Speed Record car in its shape and in its use of aerodynamic fairings ahead of and behind each wheel. Various scale models were tested in the wind-tunnel at Vickers, and the front end design was also changed to improve the aerodynamics after initial testing. The car was initially painted bright yellow, and gained the nickname of Yellow Canary, but by late 1931 its colour appears to have been changed to orange. The engine was similar to the Ulster racing type, and was first tried with a Zoller supercharger, although the Racing Department later replaced this with an Austin-built Roots type unit. Power was 56bhp at 6000rpm.

Its first public outing was at Brooklands in May 1931, when it completed only one lap. At the August Bank Holiday meeting it achieved 99.64mph; then after a major engine rebuild it polished off the Mile at 100.67mph and raised the Two-way Kilometre record to 102.28mph. These figures bettered Eyston's records. Further changes moved the radiator forward under a separate cowling to improve cooling, and the car then recorded its best-known achievement at the Montlhéry track on 8 September 1931 when it broke the International Class H records in the hands of Mrs Gwenda Stewart with speeds of around 109mph.

The car broke further records at Montlhéry in the hands of Gwenda Stewart.

RUBBER DUCKS, 1931

The success of the streamliner persuaded the Racing Department to build another works team of three cars, this time to compete in the October 1931 Brooklands 500 Mile event.

These single-seater cars are generally known as the "Ducks" or "Rubber Ducks" because of the raised rear headrest on two of them which provided a profile like that of a rubber duck (the name Dutch Clog has also been used). The driver sat low down and almost over the rear axle, with an aero screen in front and the short tail with its high headrest behind. The bodies were frameless and constructed from aluminium and steel, with a large radiator cowl standing proud at the front, as on the final version of the streamliner.

The mechanical specification consisted of a supercharged Ulster-type engine with 56bhp at 6000rpm that drove through a three-speed close-ratio gearbox to a 4.5:1 rear axle. Top speed was 105mph. In the beginning, the engines had a Zoller vane-type supercharger, but during 1932 this was changed for a Roots type.

These cars took the Austin works team to victory in the JCC International Race at Brooklands on 6 May 1933. One of them was subsequently sent to New Zealand.

One of the surviving 'Rubber Duck' racers. (Matthew Barker)

The mechanical specification consisted of a supercharged Ulster-type engine with 56bhp at 6000rpm that drove through a three-speed close-ratio gearbox to a 4.5:1 rear axle. Top speed was 105mph. (Matthew Barker)

STREAMLINER, 1932

In 1932, Austin staff testing some works cars at Brooklands encountered an Ulster model which was recording faster times than their own. They approached the driver to ask about it, and discovered he was Tom Murray "Jamie" Jamieson and that the car was being tested with a supercharger that he had designed. Jamieson was then working for the supercharger specialist Amherst Villiers, but before long he was taken on by Arthur Waite at Austin and brought his designs with him. He was set to work to design the fastest side-valve Seven that he could, to meet Austin's aim of reclaiming the Class H record from George Eyston, who had recently set a new figure of 118.38mph in an MG.

The car was built with the engine from Jamieson's Ulster, which used a two-lobe Roots-type supercharger. This was initially capable of 70bhp at 8000rpm, and was later further developed to give 74.5bhp, and it drove through a three-speed Ulster gearbox. The chassis had its transmission offset to allow a low frame level, and the streamlined single-seater body was built from aluminium and had wheel fairings similar to those on the 1931 Streamliner.

The car was taken to the Montlhéry track in October 1933, where it achieved over 119mph to take the Five Miles and Ten Miles Class H records. Unfortunately this success was short-lived because MG reclaimed the record a few days later. In March 1934, the car was taken to the Speed Record Week at Southport for another record attempt, when it achieved a new Class H record for the Flying Kilometre of 122.74mph driven by Pat Driscoll. The Austin Racing Department considered that it had now reached the limit of its development as a speed record car and converted it into a track and sprint racer, when it took the new name of "No 2" (see below).

SIDE-VALVE RACERS, 1934

The side-valve racers had a distinctive profile thanks to their tall headrest fairings. The dish-like object alongside the bonnet is an air intake for the carburettor. (Matthew Barker)

Work began on the new Twin Cam racers in 1934 (see below), but to keep Austin in the limelight a new track racer was created from the earlier Jamieson streamliner. Engine and transmission went into a new frame with a tubular front axle, and a very light body was created with a bulbous nose cowling. With around 85bhp at 8500rpm on alcohol fuel, and a close-ratio four-speed gearbox, the car hit a quite sensational 140mph at Southport on 24 March 1934 in the hands of Pat Driscoll. Kay Petre was also very successful with the car, and Austin now decided to build a second car, which somewhat inevitably took the name of No 3.

This second car was built during 1934 for German driver Walter Baumer to use in continental European events, and had a longer tail and a slightly different front end. Build delays with No 3 led to No 2 being sent out to Baumer instead, and eventually Pat Driscoll took over the new car. Baumer's car was later rebodied at the Austin works in the new style established by the Grasshoppers (see below), but from 1936 it was superseded by the Twin Cam cars. No 2 still survives and was formerly part of the Donington Collection of Grand Prix cars. These cars are often known as the Side-valve Racers.

No 2 still survives and was formerly part of the Donington Collection of Grand Prix cars. (Vauxford, CC-by-SA 2.0)

GRASSHOPPERS AND LE MANS SPORTS, 1935-1937

Between 1935 and 1937, Austin built a group of cars that were intended for reliability trials rather than speed events, as it was clear that the Seven was no longer competitive there. These cars were initially known as the Grasshoppers, and from them were developed a group of cars designed to compete in the Le Mans 24 Hour event.

A first car was built in 1934, and then three more were built in early 1935 to compete in the MCC Lands End Trial, where they were successful. These were described as Speedy models, but they had 6-gallon rear tanks to which were mounted twin spare wheels, plus a radiator grille with vertical central bar. The engines were two-bearing types with pressure lubrication, but as power was increased during the season the crankshaft gave trouble. This was partly cured with a special Laystall crankshaft.

Four more cars in the series were built in early spring 1935 for the Le Mans 24 Hour race. They had similar bodies but with cycle-type wings, and they had Jamieson-designed aluminium cylinder heads. They were not successful at Le Mans: two cars retired, and the other two finished 27th and 28th out of the 28 finishers.

On return to Longbridge, they were re-equipped for reliability trials, and in these events they performed reasonably well but clearly lacked power. One was supercharged with great success for the 1936 Colmore Trial, and the others were then also fitted with Centric Type 125 superchargers, accompanied by a large SU carburettor which necessitated an ugly bonnet bulge. These supercharged two-bearing engines would rev to 7000rpm and power the cars to around 80mph.

A final batch of four cars was prepared for the 1936 Le Mans event. These were very similar to the 1935 Le Mans cars but had no doors (to save weight) and now had unsupercharged three-bearing engines with enlarged water passages in a block that was taller than standard to accommodate unusually long valves. The 1936 Le Mans entry was cancelled because of industrial unrest, and so the cars were held over for the 1937 Le Mans. Only three of the cars were entered, now modified with 4.00 tyres on 17in wheels to improve roadholding. However, all three had to retire when the oil feed to the centre main bearing failed.

The cars were rebuilt and entered for the 12hr Sports Car race at Donington, where they finished second, third and fifth. One was later entered for the September 1937 Paris-Nice Rally by Kay Petre and a French lady driver. As for the fourth of this last batch of Le Mans cars, it was eventually sold to a privateer in Ulster.

Several of these cars still survive, although some are no longer in their original form.

The first Grasshoppers were built to compete in reliability trials rather than speed events,

TWIN-CAM RACERS, 1935

By late 1934 it was clear that the Seven's side-valve engine had reached the limit of its development for speed and competition work. Sir Herbert Austin gave his approval to development of a new racing machine to contest the 750cc class in which the Seven had been dominant for so long, and Murray Jamieson was given a free hand to design it.

Jamieson's original idea for a 1500cc mid-engined V8 nevertheless did not impress Sir Herbert, and the car was redesigned around a new conventionally located 744cc block with twin overhead camshafts and a Roots-type supercharger. This developed 116bhp at 9000rpm. The car sat on an 82in wheelbase and in outline was similar to the last of the side-valve racers, with a short tail that also formed the driver's headrest. There was a 25-gallon fuel tank but no mechanical pump was fitted, and a hand pump was therefore fitted outside the bodywork so that the driver could pressurise the tank as needed while racing. However, the Twin-Cam racers incorporated no Austin Seven production components except for the clutch cover.

The first trial run was at Donington in October 1935 and was successful. Two more cars were then built to complete the planned team of three. The car was publicly announced in March 1936, and was subsequently used to recapture some records from MG, although Jamieson was disappointed that it did not quite achieve his 120mph design target. He later left Austin and joined ERA.

The first competitive outing was at the Brooklands Easter meeting in 1936, when the car was not a big success. Subsequent modifications improved both power and reliability, and the Twin Cam cars had successful seasons in 1937 and 1938, latterly with modified bonnet styling. They continued to race successfully into 1939, by which time of course the Austin Seven that had been their inspiration had ceased production. One Twin Cam racer survived in the now-disbanded Donington Collection of Grand Prix Cars.

The Twin-cam racers were perhaps the ultimate evolution of the racing Seven. (Matthew Barker)

OVERSEAS MANUFACTURE

Overseas demand for the Austin Seven led to a number of special variants that were actually created outside Britain. Australia received large numbers of bare chassis that were bodied by its own domestic coachbuilders in a variety of (typically sporting) styles. Licence agreements with France, Germany, Japan and the USA allowed local manufacture to Austin patents, and inevitably there were further developments of the basic designs to suit local requirements. These arrangements also prolonged the production life of the Seven: although the last cars were built in Britain in 1939, the last derivatives from Rosengart in France were not built until 1953.

AUSTRALIA

Exports of fully-built Austin Sevens to Australia began in 1923, but were never very numerous because of high import taxes. The Australian government had imposed these taxes in 1912 to protect the local coachbuilding industry, and the way around them was to export bare chassis to be bodied locally in Australia. So from 1925 Austin did exactly that.

Coachbuilding for imported chassis had become a big business in Australia by the 1920s, and there were multiple practitioners of the art, both large and small. However, by the middle of the decade it was Holden Motor Bodies who had the lion's share of the business. In 1924, the company built no fewer than 22,150 bodies to 65 different designs and for a wide variety of chassis at its newly-opened plant in Woodville, South Australia. It was Holden who became Australia's largest maker of bodies for the Austin Seven, but it was far from the only one and several smaller companies made their own contributions.

This section of the catalogue is arranged alphabetically by the name of the coachbuilder.

CONOULTY

Bill Conoulty raced motorcycles before turning to cars and obtained an Austin agency in Sydney in 1927. He began racing competitively in 1929 and developed several performance modifications for the Austin Seven. Among these were overhead camshaft and overhead valve conversions, and a special cylinder head which he described as the Cushioned Power type. Conoulty was well known for his Comet racer, which was also called the Conoulty Special Austin Comet.

Bill Conoulty doing some last minute repairs on his Austin 7 Comet Racer in October 1946. (Mitchell Library, State Library of New South Wales)

GREEN

William Green of Parramatta Road, Petersham in Sydney was another of the many Australian coachbuilders to work on the Austin Seven chassis. His company is known to have created at least two designs, one a leather-panelled Sportsman Coupé and the other a jaunty little two-seater Sports that was known as the Wasp. (The Wasp was incorrectly attributed to Melbourne Motor Body Works and given a date of 1927 in Bryan Purves' *Austin Seven Source Book.*)

Characteristics of the Wasp were a fashionable shovel-shaped radiator cowl that could be painted in the body colour or plated to choice, and a spare wheel that was carried on the driver's side of the body where a door would otherwise have been. There is no clear information about the quantities built or the build dates, but the period from 1928 to 1930 has been suggested and at least one surviving example is known to have been built in early 1929.

HOLDEN

1928 Holden Roadster..

1928 Holden Family Tourer. (Cars Down Under)

Holden began making bodies for imported Austin chassis in 1925, and the company's most numerous products were Tourer and Roadster types. The Holden connection appears not to have been highlighted in advertising; these were simply Austin Sevens with all-steel bodies made in Australia.

The Holden Family Tourer was very similar to the contemporary British Chummy but had a raised moulding around the body just below waist height and a visible join below each door where the steel body met the aluminium scuttle supplied with the chassis. There was also a Roadster body, essentially an open two-seater with a folding top and a quite capacious projecting boot that was accessible from inside the body and could be locked. Many Roadsters appear to have been built for government and other official bodies.

A series of new body designs appeared in 1935, with the sloping radiator grille and valanced wings introduced by the Ruby. These all came with 18in wire wheels with 4in wide tyres. They included a Sports Tourer, a Roadster (with a De Luxe variant), a Coupé

and a Utility (or pick-up truck). The Coupé was very American in appearance; the Utility was a characteristically Australian body style favoured especially in rural communities. The 1936-1937 models of the Sports Tourer had 16in wheels with 4.75in tyres and rear-hinged doors instead of the front-hinged type on the 1935 models.

1931 Holden Saloon. (Cars Down Under)

A series of new body designs arrived in 1935 with the sloping radiator grille and valanced wings of the Ruby. This 1937 Holden Coupé was very American in appearance. (Cars Down Under)

FLOOD

James Flood was a major figure in early Australian motoring and his Melbourne coachworks bodied a number of prestigious imported chassis. The company built several designs for Austin Seven chassis, all with a deliberately sporting bent and typically with a raked steering column to allow lower lines. Flood operated a programme of continuous development and his designs evolved over the years. Many had some form of streamlined radiator cowling, but some retained the standard Austin radiator shell.

The Flood coachworks was one of the many Australian companies that built a sports two-seater known as a Meteor, in their case between 1928 and 1931. This had the short, wasp tail associated with the Meteor "brand" and also had a streamlined cowling – of which there was more than one design – ahead of the radiator. There was also a Standard Sports model in the same period, with the standard Austin radiator shell and a long bonnet with multiple louvres. Both the Meteor and the Standard Sports had a spare wheel mounted on the body side next to the driver, and a single door on the passenger's side.

The Flood Coupé had a variation on the popular reverse-rake cowled radiator grille.

There was also at least one design of coupé body in this period, with a door on each side. The Flood bodies continued to be produced into the mid-1930s.

The Standard Sports design from James Flood seems to have been shared with Latrobe. Flood was calling it the Austin Ace model by the time of this 1933 example, and that name is on the grille badge. (Cars Down Under)

LATROBE

Latrobe Body Works was a Melbourne coachbuilder that sold direct to the public through its own showrooms. Its 1927 Tourer body for the Seven was very similar to the contemporary Chummy, even though the company claimed to have made 23 improvements over the British-built model! Early doors were square but hindered access to the rear seats, so later bodies had an angled trailing edge.

The company also offered a Sports Seven from 1927 to 1930, which had aluminium panels over an ash frame. This two-seater had a raked steering column, cycle wings, a neatly tapered tail and an impressively louvred bonnet, while the spare wheel was carried outside the body beside the driver. The exhaust ran along the left side of the car outside the bodywork and there was a simple folding hood.

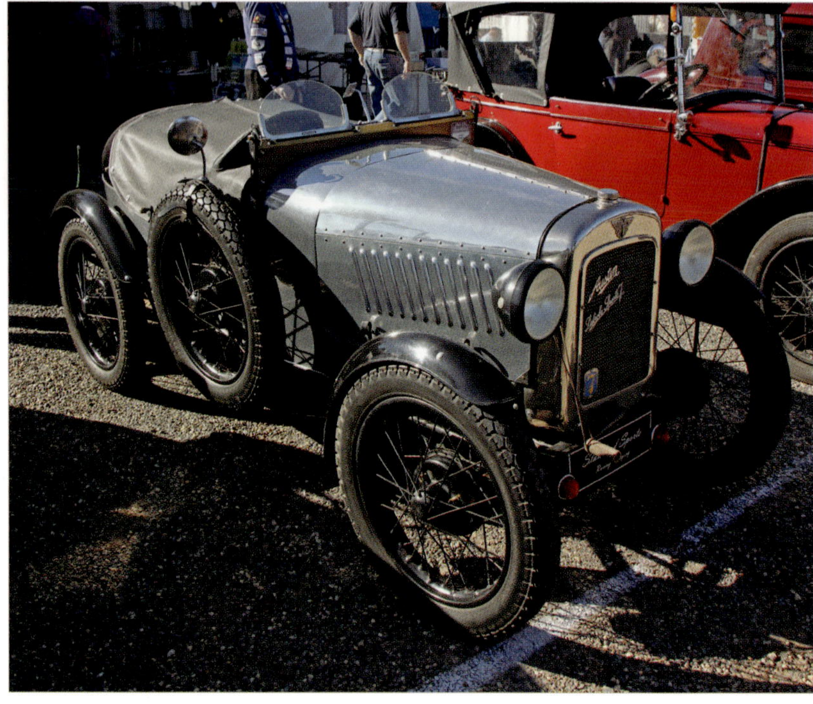

The grille badge here reads "Latrobe Sports 7", and the two-seater body is very similar to that built by James Flood. (Cars Down Under)

LONZAR

Just three Lonzar Meteors were built, all in 1930.

Jack Lonzar ran a small coachbuilding business in Adelaide, South Australia, and built another variation on the Meteor sports theme. His design had the usual wasp tail and radiator cowling, with cycle wings and the spare wheel carried outside the body alongside the driver. The chassis was a standard production Austin Seven of the time, with its steering column lowered and lengthened.

Three Lonzar Meteors were built, all in 1930.

NEW SOUTH WALES MOTORS

New South Wales Motors of Sydney were probably first off the mark in Australia with a special body for the Austin Seven. In 1924, they produced the Austin Seven Ace, a steel-panelled sporting two-seater with louvred bonnet sides and "aerodynamic" radiator cowling. The windscreen folded forwards for competition work, but there is no information about what, if anything, was done to the engine. Production numbers are also unknown.

RICHARDSON

The Richardson Body Works of Sydney, New South Wales, offered their take on the Meteor sports design from 1928. This had the usual short wasp tail and streamlined radiator cowling, and the body had aluminium panels, a spare wheel carried outside the body alongside the driver, and a vee screen that was permanently attached to the scuttle.

The general design of the Meteor sports two-seater was shared by several coachbuilders, who all used the Meteor name. This one was built by Richardson in Sydney.

ROBINSON

A Robinson & Co was another Sydney coachbuilder who produced a sports model called the Meteor. Their version was available from 1928-1929 and was based on the AD Tourer chassis, with a more steeply raked and lengthened steering column. The body had metal panels with the usual wasp tail and cowled radiator; 1928 models had two doors but the 1929 Robinson Meteor had only a passenger's side door and its spare wheel mounted outside the body on the driver's side. Only small numbers were made.

This interpretation of the Meteor came from Robinson who, like Richardson, was based in Sydney. (Christopher Killalea, CC-by-SA 3.0)

SYKES

The Sykes Moth was another example of a dedicated sports body for the late-1920s Seven. It was made by Geo Sykes of Gordon Road, Chatswood in Sydney, and featured a reverse-sloped grille cowl, minimal two-seater bodywork panelled in aluminium, and a spare wheel that was carried outside the body on the driver's side. It is not clear how many were made.

Broadly similar to the Wasp and the Meteor, the Moth was another two-seater Sports from a Sydney coachbuilder, in this case Sykes. (Cars Down Under)

FRANCE

The engineer Lucien Rosengart resigned as the Managing Director of Peugeot in May 1928, recruited designer Jules Salomon (responsible for the first Citroën) and set up a new company in his own name in a factory at Neuilly-sur-Seine that he bought from his former employers. His objective was to produce a small car for a market demand that he believed was not being met by the major French car makers.

He quickly signed an agreement with Austin to build the Seven, initially to the Austin designs but with the freedom to make progressive changes to suit his target market. In practice, Austin supplied 100 CKD sets from which the first Rosengart chassis were built in June 1928, with locally designed and manufactured bodies. Rosengart called his model the 5CV (5 fiscal horsepower by the French rating system) and always supplied it with right-hand drive. As soon as French manufacture began in late 1928, however, he switched to metric fixings and French-made Ducellier electrics, with footbrake-operated brakes on all four wheels and some minor differences in the manufacture of the Austin engine.

The Rosengart 5CV gradually began to incorporate more and more differences from the parent Austin Seven. When the initial LR2 series gave way to the LR4 in 1931, the design was already quite different from its British contemporary, with a wheelbase of 2200mm (86.6in) and semi-elliptic rear springs. Further major changes in 1936 brought the Rosengart Supercinq (super Five) range that lasted until 1940, and from 1937 the bore and stroke of the Austin-designed engine were changed to improve output. Yet despite satisfactory sales of the 5CV and of other Rosengart models, profit margins were slim and by 1936 Rosengart was in trouble. Its founder transferred the company to a new organisation, Societé Industrielle de l'Ouest Parisien, and retired.

The early Rosengart was recognisably related to the contemporary Austin Seven, although wheel discs gave it a rather more substantial and modern appearance.

After the war, when attempts to sell a larger-engined car came up against economic reality, the Rosengart company returned to making small cars with a new range introduced in 1952 that revitalised the company's own version of the Austin engine and had left-hand drive. However, it was underpowered by the standards of the time, and these final descendants of the Rosengart 5CV did not sell well. The company had already filed for bankruptcy in 1952 and closed temporarily. With a stay of execution it began production again in 1953, but finally succumbed in 1955.

A Rosengart-built LR2 engine. (Matthew Barker)

ROSENGART LR2 MODELS, 1928-1931

The first Rosengart 5CV models were announced at the Paris Salon in 1928 and were known as LR2 types. Their chassis conformed to Austin specifications except where French components were used, and all models had spun aluminium discs covering their wire wheels. The French-built range of bodies had steel panels on ash frames, and consisted of a Cabriolet, a Two-seater, a Van, a Saloon and a Coupé. A second style of Coupé was added in October 1928, and this range continued into 1930, by which time around 11,000 cars had been made.

The Cabriolet was a three-seater with transverse rear seat and an external rear luggage locker with the spare wheel mounted on it. The saloon had a similar rear locker and spare wheel arrangement. The Two-seater and the Coupé shared a design with a neatly curved rear end, the Coupé of course having a fixed roof and door tops. The Van had shorter doors than the saloon but a similar profile.

This initial range was joined in October 1928 by a Type B Coupé, with cramped 2+2 seating made possible by using a folding luggage rack instead of a closed locker. This body had an attractive contrast between its painted aluminium lower panels and fabric-covered upper panels. Some rarities from the following year included a Coupé de Ville body and a quite remarkable full-width "tank" body for a two-seat torpedo model that was bodied by Busson.

From 1930, Rosengart extended the chassis rearwards over the back axle to allow more room in the bodies, and also to allow longer semi-elliptic leaf springs to be fitted, and that year the company also began to make Sports models for competition use. These seem to have been made to order and in consequence there was no standardised design. Some seem to have been fitted with Type EA engines, gearboxes and rear axles imported from Britain.

A 1930 Rosengart LR2 Coupé. (Clive Barker)

A 1930 Rosengart LR2 Van. (Clive Barker)

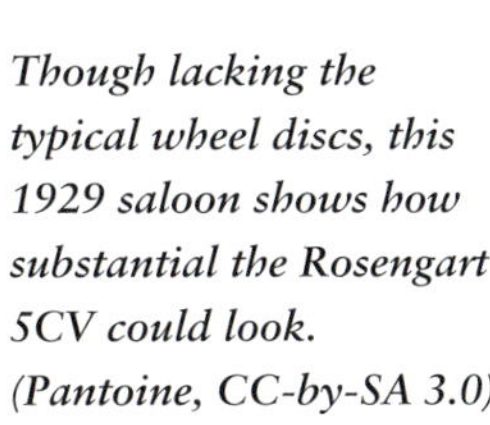

Though lacking the typical wheel discs, this 1929 saloon shows how substantial the Rosengart 5CV could look. (Pantoine, CC-by-SA 3.0)

Busson's 1929 "tank" body for the 5CV made the car look toy-like – which was probably the intention.

ROSENGART LR4 MODELS, 1931-1935

In 1931 the original LR2 range gave way to a new type called the LR4. This departed further from the contemporary Austin specification, and its chassis now had a longer 2200mm (86.6in) wheelbase. The rear axle was now of Rosengart design as well as manufacture. The initial LR4 types were Saloons, with a top-opening rear locker, and remained in production until 1933.

From 1933, the range expanded yet again, notably with a wider range of light commercial models. There were longer wheelbases again: 2300mm (90.5in) for the LR44 saloon and cabriolet models, and 2600mm (102.3in) for the LR45 type that underpinned the Commerciale Rural six-window saloon (where the rear body doubled as a travelling salesman's van) and the Fourgon van, which could have roll-up canvas instead of metal panels in the rear to create a mobile shop display for tradesmen who frequented the country markets. The 2200mm wheelbase meanwhile remained for the LR49 chassis of 1934, with cabriolet, two-door saloon ("coach") or aerodynamic saloon bodies that lasted until at least 1936. A 2350mm (92.5in) wheelbase was created for the LR47E chassis used for a range of four-door saloons – probably the only ones ever built on a chassis related to the Austin Seven – available between 1933 and 1935.

This 1933 Rosengart LR4 Saloon belongs to the Mawby collection. (Clive Barker)

An unrestored 1933 Rosengart LR4 Van (Clive Barker)

ROSENGART SUPERCINQ, 1936-1940

French style: this is the rear of a preserved Supercinq Coupé. (Cjp-24, CC-by-SA 4.0)

Staying with the 2200mm wheelbase, the next series of Rosengart models arrived in 1936 as the Supercinq or LR 4N2 range. From the start, these were very different from the contemporary Longbridge product, with very different front-end panels, perforated disc wheels, and of course bodies designed to suit French tastes and practices. There was a wide variety of cabriolets, coupés and saloons, some with an extra-large boot, plus Commerciale and new van models. During 1937, the engine was revised with a narrower 55.9mm bore while retaining the original 76.2mm stroke, which allowed it to rev higher and reach peak power at 3800rpm. Still fiscally a 5CV, it now also came with a four-speed gearbox.

The Supercinq range lasted until 1940, when a revised LR 4N2A chassis was introduced, together with LR 4R1 and LR 4R1.1 types. But the German occupation of France threatened production from June 1940, and although a 1941 model with the LR 4R1.2 chassis did enter production, few were made.

The Supercinq had lost all family resemblance to the Seven on which it was based. This is a 1938 LR4 N2 Coupé model. (Croquant, CC-by-SA 3.0)

ROSENGART POST-WAR MODELS, 1952-1953

When Rosengart's attempts to sell larger cars foundered in the late 1940s, the company resurrected its modified Austin engine, had a modern all-enveloping body designed by Philippe Charbonneaux, and introduced the result at the 1952 Paris Salon. Alongside the

Ariette saloon were two-door Coach, Cabriolet and Break (estate car) derivatives, but all were priced way out of their market and failed to sell. A stripped-down Artisane version at a cheaper price in 1953 was still too expensive, and these cars became the last Seven derivatives produced by Rosengart. They were virtually unrecognisable as descendants of the original models from 1927.

The post-war Ariette saloon may have had an engine derived from the original Seven type, but visually it was worlds away from the Austin original. (Clive Barker)

GERMANY

The first company to take out a manufacturing licence for the Seven in Germany was the Dixi Werke in 1927. Dixi was sold to BMW in 1928, and BMW continued to develop the car until 1932. Coachbuilder, Ihle, built special bodies on existing Dixi or BMW chassis from 1933.

The German market also received left-hand-drive Austin models in the early 1930s, through the intermediary of a British company, Willys-Overland Crossley, which had a branch in Berlin. The Longbridge factory supplied RL Saloons with left-hand drive, and subsequently shipped right-hand-drive RP types that were converted to LHD in Berlin. During 1933 there were also some left-hand-drive Nippy models for Germany. However, Willys-Overland Crossley entered voluntary liquidation later that year, and closed down in 1934. A number of left hand drive Austins featuring Willys-Overland Crossley name plates have shown up over the last few years that suggest manufacturing of the left hand components (at least) continued as late as 1938.

DIXI

The entrepreneur and speculator Jakob Schapiro made his fortune in the early years of the 20th century by buying into several German car companies and establishing dealerships to sell the cars. In 1904, he established the Dixi Werke at Eisenach and from 1927 took out a manufacturing licence for the Austin Seven. However, as the financial situation in Germany stabilised in the mid-1920s, Schapiro's business model collapsed and in 1928 he was receptive to an offer from BMW to purchase the Dixi Werke.

Dixi had decided to move into the small-car market when the difficult economic climate of 1920s Germany caused sales of its existing cars to falter. The quick solution was a licensing agreement with Austin to build the Seven, and the initial agreement was for 2000 cars a year. Austin received a royalty for each car that was built.

The lines of this 1928 DA-1 Tourer are readily recognisable as those of the Austin Seven. (Matthew Barker)

Austin supplied the first 100 cars as kits for assembly in Germany, between February and May or June 1927. These were predominantly AD Tourers but also included Saloons, Two-seaters and Vans. However, by December 1927 Dixi had tooled up to build the cars itself to Austin designs. These were adapted to use metric fixings, Bosch electrical components, and left-hand drive. The cars went on sale in January 1928 and were known as DA-1 types, those letters standing either for Dixi-Austin or Deutsche Ausführung (German edition), and were marketed as 3/15 models. The 3 indicated the 3PS taxation class and the 15 represented the engine's horsepower.

The DA-1 bodies were built for Dixi by Mercedes-Benz in Sindelfingen, near Stuttgart, about 200 miles south-west of Eisenach. The DA-1 Phaeton was essentially an AD Tourer, and the Limousine (saloon) and Zweisitzer (Two-seater) were also very much in the mould of the parent Seven. A number of Two-seaters were delivered to the German Army, where some were stripped down and fitted with dummy tank bodies for training purposes; at this stage, the German Army was still forbidden by the Treaty of Versailles to have any real tanks. Dixi also made bare chassis available to coachbuilders, and among those who constructed bodies was Buschel (about whom very little is known), who built a small number of Cabriolets in 1928.

The Dixi DA-1 sold very well. Although only 42 cars were actually built in 1927, the overall total built by the company is claimed to have been 4831.

BMW

BMW took over the Dixi Werke and all its assets on 1 October 1928, and probably intended from the beginning to gain experience of car manufacture from the DA-1 to help in developing its own car. Manufacture continued at the Eisenach works, and the largely unaltered DA-1 became a BMW 3/15. In that guise, it remained in production until late 1929, but by then BMW had already developed its own improvements to the design and the new DA-2 model had gone on sale alongside the last of the old types.

The DA-2s were introduced in April 1929, and came as Two-seaters, Cabriolets, Phaetons, Limousines and Military personnel cars. BMW's chief engineer Max Friz had designed larger doors for all models to improve access. He had also introduced lower overall gearing to improve acceleration and had arranged for the footbrake to operate on all four wheels rather than just the rear pair. The DA-2 Two-seaters were lighter than their predecessors; the new Cabriolet was in much the same mould but with fixed frames around its full-height doors; and the Phaeton was similar to the AE Tourer version of the parent Seven but had the new longer doors.

The Military personnel car was based on the Phaeton and was intended for reconnaissance duties. All had special stowage in the rear, some had cycle-type front wings, and most if not all had a machine-gun mount on the scuttle. They also had 19in wheels rather than the 27in size of the civilian models. Meanwhile, the Limousine brought some major changes. It had a longer and higher bonnet than the other DA-2 models, and its all-steel body was built by Ambi-Budd in Berlin and came with a neat luggage locker at the rear. It was wider than other bodies and so had no running-boards (although a set could be ordered at extra cost). There was also a Sonnenscheinlimousine (Sunshine Saloon) derivative, which differed only in having a roll-back roof.

The range of bodies was expanded from the original five to eight in 1930, with a four-seater Cabriolet that had a luggage boot like the saloon (and was possibly also built by Ambi-Budd), an attractive two-seater Coupé with a neatly curved boot accessible from inside the car, and a Delivery Van. All these remained available into 1931. Production totals claimed for the DA-2 include 6600 Phaetons, 1387 Two-seaters,

This DA-2 Cabriolet dates from 1930. (BMW)

The DA-2 Zweisitzer (two-seater) had sidescreens instead of winding windows in the doors.

A 1929 DA-2 3/15 Limousine. (Clive Barker)

Ambi-Budd built the Saloon body on this 1931 DA-2 model. Disc covers over the wire wheels give the car a more solid air.

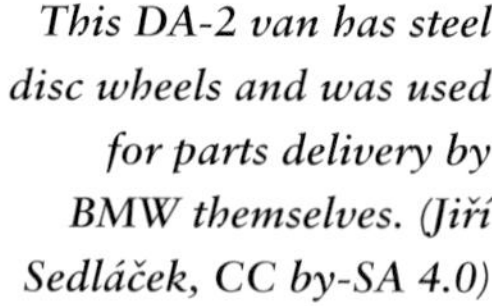

This DA-2 van has steel disc wheels and was used for parts delivery by BMW themselves. (Jiří Sedláček, CC by-SA 4.0)

1374 Cabriolets, 435 Delivery Vans, and 300 Cabriolets. There were also some bare chassis: one went to the Berlin coachbuilder Buhne, who had also built bodies for the earlier Dixi 6PS models, and who constructed a neat four-seat 3/15 cabriolet for the 1931 Berlin Motor Show.

Meanwhile, January 1930 brought yet another new model, which was different enough from the others to be given the new designation of DA-3. This was a dedicated sporting model, intended for both private and "works" competition. It also carried the name of Wartburg, which was the name of the mediaeval castle on one of the hills overlooking the town of Eisenach where the factory was situated.

The DA-3 Wartburg had a boat-tailed two-seater body and a more powerful engine, which developed 18bhp at 3200rpm thanks to a side-draught Solex carburettor and a special head gasket that raised the compression ratio to 7:1. The cars came with either 19in wheels (with 3.5in tyres) or 18in wheels (with 4in tyres) and a drop-centre front axle. There even appears to have been some support from Austin, who supplied some racing engines from Longbridge. Production lasted into 1932, and a total of 150 examples were built. Many were used quite successfully in German club events during the 1930s.

For the final iteration of the licence-manufactured Seven, BMW were even more ambitious. This took the name of DA-4, was introduced in January 1931, and came with independent front suspension that had been designed by Max Friz. This was not particularly sophisticated, and still depended on a transverse leaf spring, but it was another step towards BMW's own car that would arrive just over two years later.

The DA-4 came as a Limousine (saloon), a Two-seater, a Phaeton (tourer), a Coupé, a Cabriolet or a Delivery Van. The Limousine body was still made of steel, but no longer had a boot and had wheel discs as standard; it was generally very similar to contemporary Seven saloons, although the scuttle was squarer. The Coupé had an attractively sloping rear end, and the Delivery Van could be had with Michelin disc wheels or the wire-spoked type used on other models. The disc-wheeled Coupé built in 1932 by Ambi-Budd appears to have been on

Starting from Tallinn in Estonia, Max Rudat drove his car to 52nd place in the 1930 Monte Carlo Rally

one of these chassis (albeit equipped with right-hand drive), but probably remained unique.

Production of the DA-4 range was halted in February 1932 to make way for the new car that BMW had designed themselves, called the 3/20. BMW negotiated an end to their contract with Austin. Production figures claimed are 2575 Limousines, 475 Two-seaters, 210 Coupés, 175 Phaetons, and unknown quantities of the other models.

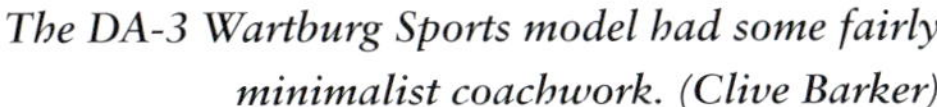

The DA-3 Wartburg Sports model had some fairly minimalist coachwork. (Clive Barker)

IHLE

The Ihle brothers created a probable total of 200 sporting machines by re-bodying Dixi and BMW DA chassis. Their coachworks was established at Bruchsal near Karlsruhe in southern Germany in 1930, and from 1933, they began to focus specifically on creating more stylish and sporting bodywork for mundane small cars. Their first success came with an all-steel design for the DA chassis. Customers could buy a kit to convert their own vehicles or could have their cars rebodied in Bruchsal. The Ihle brothers also sold complete cars, created from second-hand vehicles that they had overhauled mechanically and rebodied.

This first DA derivative was called the Ihle Sport Type 600, was always painted bright red and boasted cycle wings and a sporty, pointed tail. Although the front axle was moved 3in forwards to allow a more steeply raked steering column, the engines were not specially tuned. They were successful enough for the Bruchsal factory to set up a special production line for the bodies in 1934.

As Ihle became more ambitious, the company's conversion work often went beyond a straightforward rebody to include new fittings and sometimes even a lengthened chassis or an uprated engine. Some bodies were custom-built. In 1936, the company introduced its Sport Type 800 body, with a longer tail carrying the externally mounted spare wheel, which could be adapted to suit DKW, Hansa or Ford Eifel chassis as well as the DA. As before, the favoured style was based on archetypal racing and sports designs, often recalling those of the 1920s. Ihle continued to offer these conversions until 1941.

Ihle based some attractive sports specials on the Dixi chassis, in this case a 1930 DA-4 model. (Rudolf Stricker, CC by-SA 3.0)

The Ihle designs featured a quite dramatically sloping tail, seen here on an 800 model.

Dixi & BMW DA Models Technical Specifications

Engine: Four-cylinder side-valve, CR 5.6:1, 15bhp at 3000rpm (DA-3 has 7:1 and 18bhp at 3500rpm)

Capacity: 748ccc

Bore x stroke: 56mm x 76.2mm

Induction: 1934-35: Zenith type 26VA carburettor; 1935-39: Zenith type 26

Power: 1934-36: 3bhp at 2400rpm; 1936-39: 17bhp at 2400rpm
21bhp at 4400rpm (Nippy),
23bhp at 4800rpm (Speedy)

Gearbox: Three-speed and reverse manual Dixi 4.9:1, 9:1, 16.1:1, rev 21.1:1

Axle ratio: 4.9:1 (DA-1); 5.35:1 (DA-2 to DA-4)

Brakes: Drums all round; footbrake operates rear pair only on DA-1

Steering: Worm and peg

Front suspension: Beam axle with transverse leaf spring (DA-1 to DA-3), IFS with leading arms and transverse leaf spring (DA-4)

Rear suspension: Beam axle with quarter-elliptic leaf springs

Wheels and tyres: 26in wheels with 3in wide tyres (DA-1) – later 3.5in

27in wheels with 4in wide tyres (DA-2 to DA-4)

Length: 152in

Wheelbase: 75in

Width: 63in

Front Track: 40in/1016mm

Rear Track: 43in/1092mm

Weight:1036-1179 lb (470-535kg) depending on model. 882 lb (400kg) for DA-3

Dixi and BMW DA models Production totals

Year	Model	Total
1927	Austin Seven	100
	Dixi DA-1	24
1928	Dixi DA-1	6120
1929	BMW Dixi DA-1	3146
	BMW DA-2	5350
1930	BMW DA-2	6702
	BMW DA-3	90
1931	BMW DA-2	646
	BMW DA-3	60
	BMW DA-4	2621
1932	BMW DA-4	480
	Grand total	23,357

JAPAN

Datsun is the first name that comes to many people's lips when discussing Japanese-built Austin Sevens. Common myth has it that Datsun built the Austin Seven either with or without a license from Austin.

The Datsun Model 11 combined ideas from several economy cars of the time, including the Austin Seven. This is a Phaeton. (HKT3012, CC by-SA 4.0)

Datsun (now more commonly known as Nissan) did build small cars in the 1930s with some similarities to the Seven, and Austin even bought one in 1935, bring it home to examine it to check it wasn't infringing any Austin patents. However, the resemblance was superficial and the two cars didn't resemble each other than any other small cars of the period. When asked about his influences, Noriyoshi Gotoh, the designer of the Datsun prototype, clarified that it was not based on the Austin Seven. Instead, he mentioned a 750cc French car called the Benjamin, with a gearbox in unit with final drive, which he had studied closely. Nissan has also emphasised:

"Nissan did not use any Austin engines, chassis or other mechanical parts in pre-war Datsuns. Nor did Nissan have any kind of licensing agreement with the Austin Motor Company before the Second World War."

However, there were Austin Sevens built and sold in Japan. Austin's Japanese importer took delivery of some 300-500 chassis in the mid-1930s. These chassis appear to have been specially adapted to the Japanese market, with a short wheelbase and narrow track to conform to Japan's smaller car classes and favourable taxation. These chassis were bodied by local coachbuilders (perhaps the same firms that were building bodies for Datsun?), much in the style of the Ruby, but adapted to the reduced dimensions.

USA

Despite success in selling licences for Austin Seven manufacture to the French and the Germans, Sir Herbert Austin was less successful with the Americans, and a deal with General Motors fell through when that company's shareholders voted against it. In late 1928, Austin decided to try again, and when visiting the USA as part of a delegation from the SMMT he took four sample cars to display at the New York National Automobile Show. He also took out newspaper advertisements to attract interested parties, and one contact led to the establishment of the American Austin Co in February 1929, finance coming partly from share issues and partly from Austin. Among its first acts was to secure a large disused factory at Butler in Pennsylvania.

The local manufacture agreement envisaged that chassis and engine would remain largely unchanged from their British equivalents, but that new bodies with greater appeal to American tastes were needed. The winning tender came from the Hayes Body Co, whose stylist Alex de Sakhnoffsky was already well known for his work on more glamorous American marques. By January 1930, prototypes of a Coupé, a Roadster, and a Delivery Van were ready to be shown at a hotel in New York while the National Automobile Show was on. They were a hit: dealers clamoured to become American Austin agents and supposedly more than 50,000 orders were taken in the first week. Clearly, the effects of the Depression were persuading US buyers that a small and economical car might be a good thing.

The American Austin followed the design of the British original in spirit, but incorporated several changes as well as locally-sourced ancillaries. Its engine was a mirror-image of the British type, with the manifold on the opposite side to avoid a foul with the left-hand drive steering column. The chassis was extended at the rear to provide better body support and to carry a rear bumper, and the semi-floating rear axle was very different from that on British cars. The brakes were still cable-operated but had larger 8in drums, and the wheels were 18in steel discs. As for the body, its design incorporated so much of American practice that it was barely recognisable as a relative of the Austin Seven.

1930 MODELS

Production began a few months after the prototypes had been displayed, the bodies being made by Hayes at their factory in Grand Rapids, Michigan, and delivered to the Butler factory for final assembly. Here again was another difference from the British-built Austin Seven, as

The US-built models always looked like scaled-down American cars of the time. This is a 1930 American Austin five-window Coupé. (Matthew Barker)

The Bantam name that was to come later came from the bonnet mascot. (Matthew Barker)

the American method was to weld the body and frame together. A total of 94 dealers were signed up; deliveries began in June 1930, and by the middle of the month American Austin was turning out 100 cars a day. The first Coupé delivered to a private individual went to singer Al Jolson.

Five different models were brought to market during 1930. First to enter production, in May, was a two-seat Coupé (in the American "five-window" idiom). A Roadster followed in October, with a stylish scalloped side treatment for those built with two-tone paintwork. A 5 cwt Van and a Pick-up Truck followed. The cars were briefly popular with the fashionable set, but it was not long before their diminutive size made them an object of fun. American Austin claimed to have received orders for over 184,000 examples, but by the end of the year they had sold only just over 8000.

1931 MODELS

For the following year, the company pinned its hopes on boosting sales by means of an enlarged model range. The Coupé was developed as a Business Coupé, with blind rear quarters, a single seat, and space alongside the driver to carry business samples. This went on sale in July. Also new was a Custom Cabriolet, which was not a cabriolet at all but a faux-cabriolet, with padded fabric covering and dummy landau irons on the blind rear quarters of the Business Coupé. This was hand-built, and rare. The original Coupé now came in either standard or De Luxe forms, and the Roadster was re-named the Runabout and became the year's most popular model.

Prices were slashed, too, but none of this really helped. Sales during 1931 were even worse than during the company's first year, and in early 1932 American Austin closed with 1500 unfinished cars in the factory and debts of more than $1 million.

1932 MODELS

American Austin's plight came to the attention of a young self-made millionaire called Roy S Evans, who had made his money by buying up surplus cars cheaply and selling them at a profit. He bought the stock of unfinished cars, arranged for them to be completed, and had them shipped to Florida. Here, he sold them at two-thirds of the original showroom price.

Once his original stock was exhausted, he arranged with the factory to build more cars, and at the same time had body manufacture transferred from Hayes to the main Butler plant as a way of saving costs. With sales looking healthy, he introduced some changes in July 1932. The cars were given a minor facelift and a minor mechanical overhaul.

The bonnet louvres changed from horizontal to vertical and the Coupé body was mildly revised with a taller and slightly raked windscreen. The Roadster also took on a taller windscreen. Wider tracks and a lower steering ratio were among the mechanical changes, and a new custom range was made available alongside the mainstream cars. New in July 1932 was a Suburban Coupé model, with token seating in the back for two children. This now had the name of 2.75 Series (the 2 was for Second Series; the meaning of the 75 is not at all clear). As 1932 wore on, so production at Butler was increased to 600 vehicles a month.

1933 MODELS

Evans had a Third Series drawn up for 1933, with new headlamps, a painted radiator shell, and repositioned rear lights. These were marketed as the 3.75 Series models, and consisted of three Coupés (standard, Business, and De Luxe), a Roadster, and a Panel Van with a single rear door. It was probably towards the end of the year that two more models joined the range, a Pick-up and a quite remarkable Pony Express version of it that featured a canvas tilt with zip fasteners.

A rather glamorous 1933 Roadster. Mechanical changes over the 1932 models included a belt drive for the dynamo and fan.

There were more minor mechanical changes, such as a change to a belt drive for the dynamo and fan in spring 1933. Sales held up quite well, and when the US Army took an interest in the American Austin as the basis of a small reconnaissance vehicle, a stripped-down, big-wheel Bantam Overland prototype was designed – although it remained experimental. The Bantam name, which came from the bonnet mascot already in use, would surface again later.

The influence of local styling trends is very apparent in this front view of a 1933 saloon. (Cars Down Under)

1934 MODELS

All this was not enough, however, and the American public still found it difficult to take such a small car seriously, despite its undoubted merits. Income failed to cancel out expenditure, and by June 1934 American Austin was in danger of going bankrupt yet again. What was probably the biggest factor in its survival was that the town of Butler wanted to keep the factory going in order to guarantee local employment. Evans was able to keep production running until the end of the year, and even introduced another new model to help keep sales alive. This was known as the 4.75 or Fourth Series, but its only real differences from the Third Series were the addition of safety glass and a change to angled bonnet louvres.

Things then went very quiet for a while at the end of 1934. There were no designated 1935 or 1936 models, while the company was re-organised. American Austin was liquidated during 1935, and its assets were sold in August to Roy Evans and his business partner William Ward. So keen were the Butler local authorities to keep the factory open that Evans was able to persuade them to sell him the factory, its contents, and the land on which it was built for $5000 – at a time when its actual valuation was $10 million.

During 1935, the business continued to operate as Evans Operations Inc, building new vehicles based on the existing 1934 American Austin designs.

A 1934 3.75 Series Standard Coupé.

1938 MODELS

The new company was formally incorporated as the American Bantam Co in the existing Butler premises during June 1936. Evans managed to persuade the noted coachwork designer Thomas Hibbard to join the Board of the new company, along with racing car designer Harry Miller, although it is doubtful whether either contributed much other than his name to the venture. A public fundraising campaign followed, and in the mean time Evans persuaded Alex de Sakhnoffsky to help in updating his original body design.

The new designs were introduced in October 1937 as 1938 models, and all featured a new bonnet and radiator cowl, new wings and a new rear valance. American Bantam also made a series of mechanical changes, supposedly to avoid paying further royalties to Austin in the UK. For the engine, the two main bearings (the American cars had never gone over to three) were changed from roller types to white metal. The chassis frame was strengthened; the rear axle went over to semi-elliptic springs; there were changes to the transmission, the steering and the brakes; and the cars now rode on 15in wheels.

These new models went on sale for 1938 as the Bantam 60 range. In the beginning, there were Roadster, Coupé, Panel Van and Pick-up models, and in February 1938 these were joined by a Speedster with a "Duesenberg sweep" (or scallop feature) in its side panels, and a highly distinctive Boulevard Delivery with a large box-like rear body allied to an open driving compartment. Sales were not strong, and only about 2000 vehicles were sold in the whole year. Undaunted, Bantam added a wooden-bodied Station Wagon model at the end of 1938. With a body made by the Mifflinburg Body Co, and sitting on a chassis frame that was slightly extended at the rear, this became the most expensive model in the range.

This sales brochure for the Bantam Custom Club Roadster shows how the later cars were marketed.

1939 MODELS

For 1939, Bantam reduced prices while Roadster, Speedster, Coupé and Boulevard Delivery all remained available. Now named the New 60 Series, they came with minor cosmetic changes that included fewer bonnet side louvres, and headlamps set into slightly modified front wings. The company also branched out into exports, shipping 50 chassis to Australia in February to receive locally-made bodywork.

The 1939 models were now named the 60 series and had minor cosmetic changes to the 1938 model.

1940 MODELS

New models followed for 1940, all derived from existing designs and now branded as Super 4 types. Central to them was a re-worked engine called the Hillmaster that now had three main bearings and increased bore and stoke sizes to give 819cc. There were some cosmetic changes, too, and the Boulevard Delivery models were dropped from the range. The Roadster and Speedster remained available, joined by a new Riviera four-seat Tourer convertible derived from the Speedster. There was also a Super 4 Hollywood Convertible, designed by Alex Tremulis, who was well known as the Chief Stylist for prestigious car maker Auburn-Cord-Duesenberg until that company failed in 1937.

Sales were still not good, and by summer 1940 Bantam had run out of capital. The last 141 cars from the 1940 range were sold off as 1941 models. Bantam would make no more cars but, as is well known, the company did have a resurgence of sorts when it hired Karl K Probst to draw up a design for the new US Army reconnaissance car – and that entered mass production under Willys-Overland and Ford as the Jeep.

The 1940 Super 4 Convertible Sedan model.

The 1940 Super 4 Panel Van

American Austin and American Bantam Production totals

American Austin, 1930-1935

1930	8558
1931	1279
1932	3846
1934	1057
1935	140
Total	**14,880**

American Bantam, 1938-1941

1938	2000
1939	1227
1940	800
1941	138
Total	**4165**

American Austin & American Bantam Technical Specifications

Engine: 747cc/45.6 cu in (56mm x 76.2mm) side-valve four-cylinder, CR 5.1:1, 13bhp at 3300rpm, 1940 models – 819cc/50 cu in (57.4mm x 79.4mm) side-valve four-cylinder, CR not known; 22bhp at 3200rpm

Induction: 1934-35: Zenith type 26VA carburettor; 1935-39: Zenith type 26

Gearbox: Three-speed and reverse manual gearbox designed in the USA

Brakes: Drums all round, 8in diameter

Steering: Worm and peg

Front suspension: Beam axle with transverse leaf spring)

Rear suspension: Beam axle with quarter-elliptic leaf springs. Later semi-elliptics

Wheels and tyres: 18in wheels with 3.75in wide tyres; 15in wheels from October 1937

Length: 122in (typical)

Wheelbase: 75in

Width: 53in

Height: 60½in (Coupé)

Track: 40in, 41½ in (1933)

*Weight:*1130 lb